ESSEX

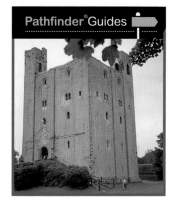

Outstanding Circular Walks

Revised by
Dennis and Jan Kelsall

Text: Original text Brian Conduit. Revised text for the 2009 edition
                      Deborah King. Revised text for the 2019 edition by Dennis
                      and Jan Kelsall.
Photography: Brian Conduit, Trotman Publishing and Peter J. Cooper.
                      Front cover: © Brian Harris/Alamy Stock Photo
Editorial: Ark Creative (UK) Ltd
Design: Ark Creative (UK) Ltd

ISBN: 978-0-31909-116-6

While every care has been taken to ensure the accuracy of the route directions, the
publishers cannot accept responsibility for errors or omissions, or for changes in details
given. The countryside is not static: hedges and fences can be removed, field boundaries
can alter, stiles can be replaced by gates, footpaths can be rerouted and changes in
ownership can result in the closure or diversion of some concessionary paths. Also, paths
that are easy and pleasant for walking in fine conditions may become slippery, muddy
and difficult in wet weather, while stepping stones across rivers and streams may become
impassable.

    If you find an inaccuracy in either the text or maps, please contact Trotman Publishing
at the address below.

First published 2001 by Jarrold Publishing.
Revised and reprinted 2005.

First published 2009 by Crimson Publishing. Reprinted with amendments in 2019.

This edition first published 2020 by Trotman Publishing.

Trotman Publishing, 19-21C Charles Street, Bath, BA1 1HX
www.pathfinderwalks.co.uk

Printed in India by Replika Press Pvt. Ltd. 6/20

Front cover: Big Essex sky and rapeseed field near Debden
Page 1: Hedingham Castle

Contents

Keymap		4
At-a-glance... walks chart		6
Introduction		8

Walks

1 Laindon Common and the Bursteads — 14

2 Waltham Abbey and the Lee Valley — 16

3 The Naze and Walton Channel — 18

4 Hanningfield Reservoir — 20

5 Chipping Ongar and Greensted church — 22

6 Thorndon Country Park — 24

7 Cymbeline Meadows and Colchester — 26

8 Finchingfield and Great Bardfield — 29

9 Mersea Island — 32

10 Weald Country Park — 34

11 Pleshey and Great Waltham — 36

12 Hatfield Forest — 38

13 St Osyth Creek — 40

14 Through the Colne Valley — 42

15 Thaxted — 45

16 Castle Hedingham and the River Colne — 48

17 Benfleet Downs and Hadleigh Marsh — 51

18 Mill Green and Blackmore — 54

19 Coggeshall and Feering — 57

20 Newport and Debden — 60

21 Stour Valley: Constable Country — 63

22 Audley Park and Wendens Ambo — 66

23 Ingatestone and Mountnessing — 69

24 Burnham and the River Crouch — 72

25 Maldon and the Blackwater Estuary — 75

26 White Notley and Cressing — 78

27 Epping Forest and Upshire — 82

28 St Peter's Chapel, Bradwell Marshes and Tillingham — 86

Further Information — 90

The National Trust; The Ramblers; Walkers and the Law; Countryside Access Charter; Walking Safety; Useful Organisations; Ordnance Survey Maps

Up to 2 ½ hours
Short walks

2 ½-3 ½ hours
Half-day walks

4 hours and over
Longer, full-day walks

The walk times are provided as a guide only and are calculated using an average walking speed of 2½mph (4km/h), adding one minute for each 10m (33ft) of ascent, and then rounding the result to the nearest quarter of an hour.

Keymap

SCALE 1:384 615 or 1 INCH to about 6 MILES *1CM to 3.8KM*

0   2   4   6   8   10 KILOMETRES   15

0   2   4   6   MILES 8   10

KEYMAP HEIGHTS SHOWN IN METRES

LONDON

Needham Market
Claydon
IPSWICH
Kesgrave
Martlesham
WOODBRIDGE
Witnesham
Grundisburgh
Lavenham
Alpheton
Long Melford
SUDBURY
Great Cornard
Hadleigh
HADLEIGH
Capel St Mary
East Bergholt
Flatford Mill
Brantham
Manningtree
Mistley
Holbrook
Chelmondiston
Shotley Gate
HARWICH
Dovercourt
Nayland
Bures
Mount Bures
Chappel
West Bergholt
COLCHESTER
Elmstead Market
WIVENHOE
Beacon End
Stanway
Aldham
Thorpe-le-Soken
Kirby Cross
WALTON-ON-THE-NAZE
FRINTON-ON-SEA
BRIGHTLINGSEA
St Osyth
CLACTON-ON-SEA
Jaywick
Holland-on-Sea
Tiptree
Tollesbury
WEST MERSEA
Mersea Flats
Colne Point
Heybridge
MALDON
Osea Island
Ramsey Island
Bradwell Waterside
Bradwell on Sea
Tillingham
Dengie Flat
Maylandsea
Latchingdon
Southminster
Burnham-on-Crouch
Foulness Sands
Foulness Point
FOULNESS ISLAND
MAPLIN SANDS
Ashingdon
Rochford
Hawkwell
Great Wakering
SOUTHEND-ON-SEA
Shoebury Ness
Gunfleet Sand
Red Sand Tower
SHEERNESS
Queenborough
Minster
Warden Point
Leysdown-on-Sea
ISLE OF SHEPPEY
Isle of Grain
Westgate on Sea
14
7
19
25
28
24
9
13
3
21

Walk	Page	Start	Nat. Grid Reference	Distance	Time	Height Gain
Audley Park and Wendens Ambo	66	Saffron Walden	TL 538385	7½ miles (12.1km)	3½ hrs	490ft (150m)
Benfleet Downs and Hadleigh Marsh	51	Salvation Army's Hadleigh Farm	TQ 808864	7½ miles (11.9km)	3½ hrs	655ft (200m)
Burnham and the River Crouch	72	Burnham-on-Crouch	TQ 952955	8½ miles (13.6km)	4 hrs	225ft (70m)
Castle Hedingham and the River Colne	48	Castle Hedingham	TL 785355	6 miles (9.7km)	3 hrs	415ft (125m)
Chipping Ongar and Greensted church	22	Chipping Ongar	TL 552031	4½ miles (7.4km)	2 hrs	270ft (80m)
Coggeshall and Feering	57	Coggeshall	TL 850226	7½ miles (12.25km)	3½ hrs	320ft (100m)
Cymbeline Meadows and Colchester	26	Cymbeline Meadows Farm Trail	TL 975259	4½ miles (7.2km)	2 hrs	220ft (65m)
Epping Forest and Upshire	82	High Beach, Epping Forest Centre	TQ 412981	8¾ miles (14km)	4½ hrs	610ft (185m)
Finchingfield and Great Bardfield	29	Finchingfield	TL 684327	4½ miles (7.3km)	2 hrs	220ft (65m)
Hanningfield Reservoir	20	Hanningfield Reservoir	TQ 737975	4 miles (6.4km)	2 hrs	300ft (90m)
Hatfield Forest	38	Hatfield Forest	TL 547202	5½ miles (8.9km)	2½ hrs	170ft (50m)
Ingatestone and Mountnessing	69	Ingatestone	TQ 651996	8¼ miles (13.25km)	4 hrs	390ft (120m)
Laindon Common and the Bursteads	14	Laindon Common (A176)	TQ 673929	3 miles (4.8km)	1½ hrs	170ft (50m)
Maldon and the Blackwater Estuary	75	Maldon, Promenade Park	TL 862064	8¾ miles (14km)	4½ hrs	355ft (110m)
Mersea Island	32	Cudmore Grove Country Park	TM 065146	5½ miles (8.9km)	2½ hrs	120ft (35m)
Mill Green and Blackmore	54	Millgreen Common	TL 639012	6¾ miles (11km)	3¼ hrs	225ft (70m)
The Naze and Walton Channel	18	The Naze car park	TM 264234	4 miles (6.4km)	2 hrs	220ft (65m)
Newport and Debden	60	Newport station car park	TL 522335	6½ miles (10.5km)	3¼ hrs	475ft (145m)
Pleshey and Great Waltham	36	Pleshey	TL 663143	5½ miles (8.9km)	2½ hrs	170ft (50m)
St Osyth Creek	40	St Osyth	TM 121155	6¼ miles (10km)	3 hrs	155ft (45m)
St Peter's Chapel, Bradwell Marshes and Tillingham	86	Tillingham	TL 992038	9¾ miles (15.6km)	4½ hrs	155ft (45m)
Stour Valley: Constable Country	63	Manningtree station	TM 094322	7¼ miles (11.75km)	3½ hrs	350ft (105m)
Thaxted	45	Thaxted	TL 611309	6 miles (9.6km)	3 hrs	335ft (100m)
Thorndon Country Park	24	Thorndon Country Park North	TQ 607914	4½ miles (7.4km)	2¼ hrs	400ft (120m)
Through the Colne Valley	42	Earls Colne High Street	TL 857289	5 miles (8km)	2½ hrs	325ft (100m)
Waltham Abbey and the Lee Valley	16	Waltham Abbey, Abbey Church Centre	TL 381007	4½ miles (7.2km)	2 hrs	90ft (30m)
Weald Country Park	34	Weald Country Park, Visitor Centre car park	TQ 568941	5 miles (8.2km)	2½ hrs	400ft (120m)
White Notley and Cressing	78	Cressing station	TL 776202	9½ miles (15km)	4½ hrs	530ft (160m)

Comments

Apart from the attractions of Saffron Walden, the route includes parkland, views of a great house and a picturesque village and church.

The walk includes grassland, woodland and marsh, and there are grand views across the Thames estuary. You can also visit a ruined medieval castle painted by Constable.

Much of the walk is beside the River Crouch and there are fine and unimpeded views across the surrounding marshland and meadowland.

There are fine views over the Colne valley, a picturesque village and the chance to visit a magnificent Norman castle.

The walk takes you through some of the pleasant and open countryside near Chipping Ongar and passes the unique wooden Saxon church at Greensted.

Coggeshall is one of the most appealing towns in Essex and there is plenty of historic interest on this walk in the valley of the River Blackwater.

From the delightful Cymbeline Meadows, the route takes you into Colchester to discover some of its historic sights, through parkland and beside the River Colne.

Apart from an incursion into open country near Upshire, the whole of this walk is through the superb woodlands of Epping Forest.

The walk takes in two exceptionally attractive villages and much pleasant countryside in between.

From several points on the walk there are fine views of Hanningfield Reservoir and across the Thames estuary to the line of the North Downs.

This easy walk in Hatfield Forest takes you through what is probably the finest surviving example of an authentic medieval forest landscape.

Two halls, three churches, a windmill and extensive views over the surrounding countryside are the main ingredients of this lengthy but undemanding walk.

A short and easy walk which starts at a surviving area of common and takes in the churches at Great Burstead and Little Burstead.

This pleasant and varied walk is almost entirely beside water and gives you the opportunity to explore the attractive old town of Maldon.

From this walk at the eastern tip of Mersea Island, there are extensive views both over the island and across the water to the Essex mainland.

The walk includes woodland and common, remnants of an ancient forest, and passes through the attractive village of Blackmore.

After walking along the cliffs of the Naze, the route turns inland and keeps along the top of an embankment, above marshes, creeks and channels, through a nature reserve.

There are fine views, both Newport and Debden are attractive villages and the route passes through parkland on the return leg.

The walk takes you through the valley of Walthambury Brook between Pleshey and Great Waltham. There is the motte of a Norman castle and defensive earthworks to see at Pleshey.

Starting from a superb monastic gatehouse, this is a walk of wide and extensive views among the creeks and marshes of the Colne estuary.

This lengthy and exhilarating walk across the lonely and desolate marshes of the Dengie Peninsula takes in two villages, two churches and a remote Saxon chapel.

This is the classic Constable Country walk on the Essex–Suffolk border that takes you through Dedham and the beautiful Dedham Vale, passing Flatford Mill and Willy Lott's Cottage.

The small medieval town of Thaxted, dominated by its magnificent church, is the focal point of this walk in the upper Chelmer valley.

The attractive woodlands of a country park are combined with open countryside and views across the Thames estuary.

Earls Colne and Colne Engaine are attractive villages with fine churches, and the walk has some wonderful views across the Colne Valley.

Starting from an impressive Norman abbey – the alleged burial place of King Harold – the walk explores the meadows, wetlands and waterways of the Lee Valley Park.

Weald Country Park provides pleasant and easy walking through woodlands, across grassland and beside a lake.

Villages, old churches and the interesting Cressing Temple are among the attractions of this walk in the pleasant landscape of the Brain valley.

Introduction
to Essex

Introduction

Although not at first glance an obvious magnet for walkers – lacking the dramatic appeal of hill-walking country – Essex does possess much fine and varied countryside. Its great expanses of lonely marshes, rolling farmlands, ancient woodlands, wide views and attractive towns and villages, more than compensate for the lack of high hills, extensive moorlands and a rugged coastline.

Unspoilt countryside

The county tends to suffer from several misconceptions and wild general-isations and three of the commonest of these – held it must be said only by those whose knowledge of Essex is fairly limited – is that it is flat, over-crowded and uninteresting.

It cannot be denied that there is a lot of flat country in Essex – as there is indeed in many other counties – but in general the landscape is best described as gently undulating. The hilliest country is in the north and west, near the Hertfordshire and Cambridgeshire borders. The county certainly suffers from the same population and traffic pressures as the other Home Counties, and many of its towns and villages have experienced substantial growth in the last two decades, but there is still plenty of open, unspoilt and tranquil countryside, especially the further away from London you get.

On the marshes of the Essex coast there is a genuine feeling of solitude and remoteness that is hard to find anywhere else in southern England. And by no stretch of the imagination can any county be dismissed as uninteresting when it possesses the oldest recorded town in Britain, some outstandingly attractive and distinctive villages and small towns, some superb medieval churches and a wealth of historic buildings, as well as much pleasant scenery and some of the finest surviving fragments of England's medieval forests.

Undulating farmland, coastal views and ancient woodland

Essex spreads northwards from the Thames Estuary to the borders of Suffolk and Cambridgeshire and eastwards from London and Hertfordshire to the North Sea coast. The coast is mainly flat, marshy and heavily indented, separated into peninsulas by broad estuaries. On the south the Thames estuary divides the county from Kent and on the north the Stour estuary is its border with Suffolk. In between are the estuaries of the Crouch, Blackwater and Colne. The extensive marshes, creeks and mudflats provide a haunting and strangely beautiful landscape of wide and unimpeded

Willy Lott's Cottage at Flatford, just over the border in Suffolk

vistas. Only in the north – at The Naze – are there cliffs and these are continually crumbling away under the onslaught of North Sea gales.

Inland the landscape is undulating and well-wooded, containing much good, fertile farmland. In the Middle Ages a large proportion of the county comprised the Forest of Essex, a vast royal hunting ground covered by dense woodland and rough heath, protected for the royal sport by a draconian code of laws. For those who infringed the forest laws punishments were severe: execution or mutilation for major offences, like killing one of the royal beasts, and fines of imprisonment for lesser crimes, such as the unauthorised felling of trees.

Over the centuries these laws lapsed and became redundant and the forest decreased in area as the mighty trees were felled and the land became converted to agricultural uses. Now only fragments remain but some of these are quite sizeable, making Essex still one of the most wooded of English counties. Most extensive and popular of these fragments is Epping Forest, a thin but long wedge of ancient woodland, covering nearly 6,000 acres (2,430 hectares) and stretching northwards from London's East End to Epping. It is a vital open space noted for its grassy plains and its superb woodlands of hornbeam, oak, beech and birch. The forest only survived further destruction as a result of prompt action by the Corporation of the City of London, which took it over by Act of Parliament in 1878 and subsequently conserved it as a recreational amenity.

Other surviving forests are Hainault, near Chigwell, bought by London County Council in 1903 and later made into a country park, and Hatfield,

In the Weald Country Park, north-west of Brentwood

near Bishop's Stortford, a National Trust property. There are smaller remnants of the forests of Writtle (near Chelmsford) and Kingswood (near Colchester), plus numerous woodlands.

On the northern fringes of Essex, near the boundaries with Cambridge-shire and Suffolk, the landscape is hillier and less wooded. This is sheep-farming country, and in the later Middle Ages this part of the county shared – along with neighbouring Suffolk – in the flourishing East Anglian woollen industry and cloth trade. This is evident in some of the small towns and villages where handsome old buildings are presided over by lofty and spacious 15th-century 'wool churches' – echoing the well-known wool churches of the Cotswolds – all built from the profits of the cloth trade. Three of the grandest of these churches are to be found at Saffron Walden, Thaxted and Dedham.

Wooden churches, estuary ports and pretty villages
In complete contrast to these magnificent wool churches, the churches in the former forested – and thus poorer – parts of the county are much smaller and plainer, often with simple wooden bell turrets instead of towers and spires. These churches are among the most charming and distinctive features of the Essex landscape. Of particular interest and appeal is the unique timber church at Greensted, near Chipping Ongar, which dates from the Saxon period.

The woollen towns of Thaxted, Dedham and Saffron Walden are among the most attractive in the county. Two others are the estuary ports of Maldon and Burnham-on-Crouch, both of which have interesting quaysides and a number of fine buildings. Pretty villages are too numerous to mention but particular mention must be made of Finchingfield, a classic English village with its combination of duck pond and old cottages presided over by a medieval church.

From Camulodunum to Audley End

It was the Saxons who gave their name to Essex but its history goes back much further. Before the Roman invasion, Camulodunum (Colchester) was a major tribal capital, referred to by the Roman writer Pliny in AD77. This is the earliest reference to any settlement in the country and Colchester can therefore claim to be Britain's oldest recorded town. After its capture it was rebuilt by the Romans as a legionary fortress and was their base for the conquest of Britain. During Boudicca's rebellion in AD60, it was sacked and burnt and had to be rebuilt, this time as a civilian settlement. Colchester still retains much of its Roman walls and possesses one of only two surviving Roman gateways in the country. A whole day could be spent wandering around this fascinating city.

After the withdrawal of the Romans, Saxon invaders penetrated the area, moving from the coast up the estuaries and on through the river valleys, to create the Kingdom of the East Saxons or Essex. Viking invaders followed, and after 1066 the Normans quickly established themselves in the area. William the Conqueror built the largest keep in England at Colchester, on the site of the Roman temple, still a most impressive sight and now housing an extensive museum. Other outstanding medieval castles are at Castle Hedingham and Hadleigh, with lesser remains at Saffron Walden and Pleshey.

The outstanding medieval timbered barns at Cressing Temple

St Osyth Priory

Essex has other associations with the Norman Conquest. At Waltham Abbey is the alleged grave of King Harold, whose body was brought here after his defeat at Hastings. The 12th-century nave of the abbey is undoubtedly the most imposing of the county's monastic remains. Others include the ruins of St Botolph's Priory in the centre of Colchester, built partly – as was much of the rest of the town – from recycled Roman bricks, and the ornate, late medieval gatehouse of St Osyth Priory, one of the finest of such structures in the country.

In the post-medieval period, as the forest was progressively cleared, conditions became more settled and agriculture prospered, a number of great country houses were built. The most impressive of these is the great 17th-century palace of the earls of Suffolk at Audley End, set in acres of attractive parkland on the edge of Saffron Walden.

John Constable, the seaside and forest recreation
One man who did more than most to put Essex on the map was John Constable, England's most famous landscape painter, although the county has to share him with neighbouring Suffolk. 'Constable Country', where the artist was born, lived and worked, is around Dedham Vale in the Stour valley, and thousands are attracted to this area on the

Audley End

Essex–Suffolk border to see the landscapes that inspired his best-known works and visit the buildings he painted.

In the Victorian railway era, a combination of sandy beaches and proximity to the capital led to the rapid growth of seaside resorts along the Essex coast at Southend, Clacton, Walton-on-the-Naze and elsewhere. Even more convenient for Londoners was Epping Forest, and regular excursions to the forest and holidays on the Essex coast became a part of the way of life for many people in London and the Home Counties.

Recently Essex has become a commuter belt and a centre for new 'hi-tech' industries, and there has been a tremendous growth of population, especially in the west of the county. However, despite these pressures, a perhaps surprisingly large amount of the older and quieter Essex still survives amid the modern bustle.

Walking in Essex

Essex is obviously not for those who are seeking dramatic landscapes or rugged hill and moorland walking. After all the highest point in the county, just outside the village of Langley – in the far north-west near the Hertfordshire and Cambridgeshire borders – only rises to 482 feet (147m). But there is more to walking than long hikes and exhausting climbs over challenging terrain, and Essex retains plenty of pleasant and unspoilt countryside, enhanced by attractive old towns, pretty villages and interesting historic monuments.

Given the nature of the terrain, the orange-coded walks in this guide – numbers 23 to 28 – are all placed in that category because of their length not because there is anything strenuous about them. Waymarking is generally good and there is an abundance of long-distance routes – Forest Way, Three Forests Way, Essex Way, St Peter's Way, Stour Valley Path, Harcamlow Way – which snake across the county and provide generally trouble free route finding. The likeliest hazards are that some of the narrow field edge and enclosed paths can become muddy in winter or after rain, and in high summer sometimes get overgrown with nettles and brambles, a relatively small price to pay for a good walk.

This book includes a list of waypoints alongside the description of the walk, so that you can enjoy the full benefits of gps should you wish to. For more information about route navigation, improving your map reading ability, walking with a GPS and for an introduction to basic map and compass techniques, read Pathfinder® Guide *Navigation Skills for Walkers* by outdoor writer Terry Marsh (ISBN 978-0-319-09175-3). This title is available in bookshops and online at os.uk/shop

Introduction

Laindon Common and the Bursteads

		GPS waypoints
Start	Laindon Common, at junction of A176 and lane to Little Burstead about 1 mile (1.6km) south of Billericay	☑ TQ 673 929 Ⓐ TQ 679 921 Ⓑ TQ 668 915 Ⓒ TQ 667 922 Ⓓ TQ 668 928
Distance	3 miles (4.8km)	
Height gain	170 feet (50m)	
Approximate time	1½ hours	
Parking	Laindon Common, off Laindon Common Road	
Ordnance Survey maps	Landranger 177 (East London), Explorer 175 (Southend-on-Sea & Basildon)	

This short walk takes you through an area of open and pleasant countryside between Billericay and Basildon, passing the church at Great Burstead and the smaller isolated church at Little Burstead. The final stretch is across the wooded Laindon Common. Some of the field paths may be muddy and overgrown.

🥾 Turn right out of the car park along a service drive to the A176. Go briefly left then carefully cross to a kissing-gate. Walk around to a yard and past farm buildings to carry on along the right-hand edge of a field.

Keep going in the same direction beside successive fields, – the tower and spire of Great Burstead church coming into view – before you eventually

Great Burstead

emerge on to a road 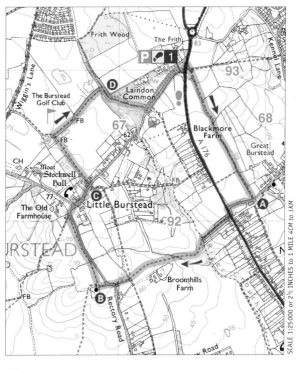. The medieval church is to the left but the route continues to the right to a T-junction. Cross the road with care and turn left, almost immediately turn right, at a public footpath sign between two houses to Little Burstead church, along a drive and continue along an enclosed path (between garden fences) which descends gently through trees and bears right to cross a footbridge over a brook. Head up an embankment to enter a field and continue across it, going over a slight brow and making for a waymarked post on the far side.

Cross a plank footbridge and, bearing right, strike out across the next couple of fields. Keep going at the edge of a third field, watching for a gap in the hedge out to a road. Turn right and, where the road bends right, keep ahead along a track to Little Burstead church.

This delightful small church has a Norman nave and the usual Essex 15th-century wooden belfry.

Immediately on entering the church-yard, turn right **B** over a stile and walk across a field, closing with the right-hand boundary beside the road and continuing in the next field. Climb out over a stile in the field corner and keep ahead along the road through Little Burstead. After 350 yards, immediately before the village hall, turn off left along a narrow enclosed path towards Wiggins Lane and Laindon Common **C**, which bends first right and then left to reach a barrier.

Pass beside it, walk along the left-hand edge of Burstead golf course and

at a hedge corner on the left, keep straight ahead to pick up and continue along the left-hand edge again. Cross a plank footbridge and immediately turn right to continue across the golf course, to the left of a hedge. Look out for where you turn right to cross a footbridge and turn left, now with the hedge on the left. In a corner at the far side of the course, go through a kissing-gate, cross a footbridge and turn right **D** along a path through the woodland of Laindon Common.

Look out for where a path leads off to the left to join another path, turn right along it and the path emerges on to a road opposite the **Dukes Head** pub. Even if you miss the path to the left, you will end up in the same place opposite the pub. Cross the road and turn left along a path through trees – parallel to the road – which leads back to the start. ●

Waltham Abbey and the Lee Valley

Start	Waltham Abbey, Abbey Church Centre	GPS waypoints
Distance	4½ miles (7.2km)	🖊 TL 381 007
Height gain	90 feet (30m)	Ⓐ TL 375 005
		Ⓑ TL 370 028
Approximate time	2 hours	Ⓒ TL 378 026
Parking	Lee Valley Park car park	Ⓓ TL 378 016
Ordnance Survey maps	Landranger 166 (Luton & Hertford), Explorer 174 (Epping Forest & Lee Valley)	

The walk takes you through part of the Lee Valley Park just to the north of Waltham Abbey, an area of grassland, marsh, lakes and waterways, largely reclaimed from gravel extraction and once the site of gunpowder works. There are attractive views across riverside meadows and most of the route is beside water. Historic interest is centred on the fine Norman abbey at the start.

🖊 Start at the Abbey Church Centre and, facing the abbey, turn right to pass under the 14th-century abbey gateway and turn left beside Cornmill Stream. Cross a footbridge and keep ahead, passing in front of the abbey.

Apart from the early 12th-century nave of an earlier church – an out-standing example of Norman archi-tecture – little else remains of the great and wealthy Augustinian abbey founded in 1177 by Henry II as part of his penance for the murder of Thomas Becket. The unfortunate King Harold is supposed to have been buried behind the high altar after his defeat and death at the Battle of Hastings in 1066, and the site of his alleged tomb can be seen to the east of the church. The abbey was dissolved by Henry VIII in 1540.

Turn right along Highbridge Street, passing the tourist information centre. Keep ahead in the Waltham Cross direction to cross High Bridge over the Horsemill Stream and after crossing a second channel – the River Lee Navigation – turn right Ⓐ at a public footpath sign, to join the towpath beside it. As you walk along, it is difficult to envisage this now green and tranquil area as once being the site of a gun-powder factory.

Continue along the towpath – passing by two locks. Keep going for another good ½ mile (800m) to a bridge Ⓑ. Leaving the towpath, cross the bridge and walk away along a tarmac path, between pools and marshland. Continue through trees and cross a footbridge to reach Hooks Marsh car park. Keep ahead over the Horsemill Stream and along a tarmac drive. Just after passing Fishers Green Farm, turn right over a stile Ⓒ. Continue along the right-hand edge of a field and, at a footpath post, turn left, in the Cornmill Meadow

Waltham Abbey

footbridge into the Abbey Grounds, keep ahead to return to the start. ●

direction, and walk diagonally across the field to come out onto a track by the corner of a high wire fence and another footpath sign.

Bear right to cross the track, keep along the right-hand field edge beside the high fence and go through a kissing-gate in the field corner. Continue along the right-hand edge of a meadow, follow the fence round to the right, and the path bears first right and then left to reach a footbridge over Cornmill Stream. Turn right over it, turn left **D** to walk along a most attractive path beside the stream, and soon the tower of Waltham Abbey can be seen across the meadows to the right.

Go through a kissing-gate and continue by the stream, curving gradually right towards the abbey. At the far end of the meadow, go through another kissing-gate and turn first right and then left to follow the path under a road. After crossing a

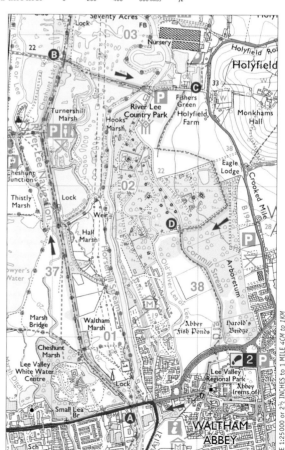

SCALE 1:25000 or 2½ INCHES to 1 MILE 4CM to 1KM

The Naze and Walton Channel

		GPS waypoints	
Start	The Naze car park, 1½ miles (2.4km) north of Walton-on-the-Naze	🖉	TM 264 234
		Ⓐ	TM 266 244
Distance	4 miles (6.4km)	Ⓑ	TM 250 248
Height gain	220 feet (65m)	Ⓒ	TM 258 228
Approximate time	2 hours		
Parking	The Naze		
Ordnance Survey maps	Landranger 169 (Ipswich & The Naze), Explorer 184 (Colchester)		

Starting by The Naze Tower, the first part of this exhilarating walk of wide vistas is along the cliffs of The Naze. You then turn away from the sea and continue along the top of an embankment above creeks, marshes, mudflats and inlets to the edge of the small resort of Walton-on-the-Naze. A final short stretch – along a road and then the coast path – brings you back to the start. Much of the route is through a nature reserve and is ideal for observing both shipping and wildlife.

The word 'naze' comes from an old English word for 'nose' and refers to the original shape of the headland. The high but crumbly cliffs – constantly being eaten away by the sea – are a rarity on the generally flat Essex coast.

🖉 Begin by heading across to The Naze Tower, built in 1720 by Trinity

Creeks near The Naze

House as a landmark, and continue northwards across the grassy clifftop, heeding the warning notices to keep well clear of the unstable edge. As the path descends to keep across the top of lower cliffs, Harwich can be seen ahead.

At one point a slight detour has to be made to the left between gorse bushes to a T-junction. Turn right, turn right again at a crossroads and immediately turn left to continue along the coast path. On joining a tarmac path, bear left **A** on to it to walk on top of an embankment, above pools and marshes and along the edge of an Essex Wildlife Trust nature reserve. Where this tarmac path ends, bear left again to continue along a pleasant grassy path – still on the top of an embankment – above Cormorant Creek and the surrounding marshland. The Naze Tower stands out prominently on the skyline to the left.

The path bends sharp left **B** to keep by the broader expanses of Walton Channel on the right and above Walton Hall Marshes on the left. A few yards before reaching a track in front of a caravan park, turn left and continue above a small pool on the right. Keep ahead to climb another one, and the path bends right to emerge on to a road on the edge of Walton-on-the-Naze **C**.

Turn left gently uphill and where the road bears left – by a sign for The Naze – continue through a small car park to join a track and then bear left on to a narrow enclosed path. At the top of steps, turn left to a track and turn right along it to return to the starting point. ●

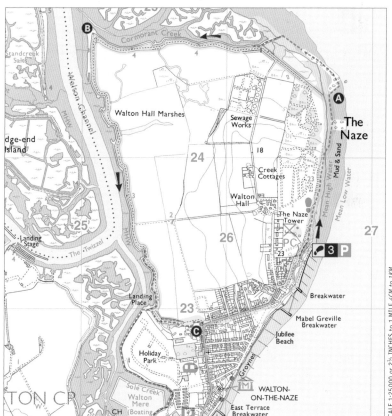

SCALE 1:25000 or 2½ INCHES to 1 MILE 4CM to 1KM

Hanningfield Reservoir

		GPS waypoints
Start	Hanningfield Reservoir, signposted from A130 to the south of Chelmsford, follow signs to Hanningfield Reservoir not the Reservoir Visitor Centre	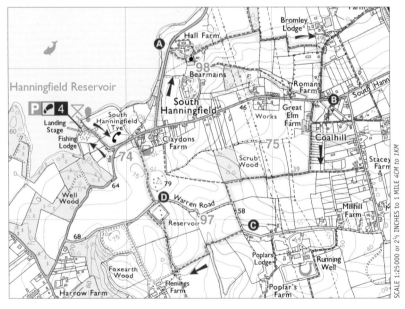 TQ 737 975
Distance	4 miles (6.4km)	**Ⓐ** TQ 742 980
Height gain	300 feet (90m)	**Ⓑ** TQ 753 977
Approximate time	2 hours	**Ⓒ** TQ 747 969
Parking	Hanningfield Reservoir	**Ⓓ** TQ 741 971
Ordnance Survey maps	Landranger 167 (Chelmsford), Explorer 175 (Southend-on-Sea & Basildon)	

The fine views over Hanningfield Reservoir – at the start and near the end of the walk – are especially welcome in an area lacking in natural lakes. In clear conditions there are also extensive views looking southwards across the Thames Estuary to the line of the North Downs on the horizon. Hanningfield Reservoir was constructed in the 1950s and is now a Site of Special Scientific Interest, renowned for its wildfowl. It is also popular for fishing and sailing.

Start by walking away from the reservoir along the drive to the road and turn left into South Hanningfield. Turn left along the road to West Hanningfield and, at a public footpath sign, turn right over a stile Ⓐ.

Walk along the left-hand edge of a field towards South Hanningfield church. The nave is Norman, the belfry was added in the 15th century and the east end was largely rebuilt in the 19th century.

Bear right, away from the field edge, to go through a kissing-gate, pass to the right of the church and head through the churchyard to a stile in the corner. Climb it, keep along the right-hand edge of the next two fields separated by a stile and, in the corner of the second one, climb two stiles in quick succession and cross a plank footbridge. Turn right along the right-hand edge of the next field, follow the edge round to the left and climb a stile. Again turn right along the right-hand field edge, follow the edge to the left and in the far corner cross a plank footbridge and climb two stiles in quick succession.

Walk across the next field, negotiate another double stile and an intervening plank footbridge and turn right along a hedge-lined track to a road Ⓑ. Turn right and, at a bridleway sign, turn left along the tarmac drive to Great Elm Farm. Where the drive turns right into the farmyard, climb the stile in front, keep ahead to cross a plank footbridge and climb a stile into a field. Walk along the right-hand field edge, negotiate a fence and keep ahead to another fence in the field corner. At the T-junction turn right along an enclosed track, continue along the left-hand edge of the next two fields, bear left through a hedge gap in the corner and walk along the right-hand edge of the next field alongside Scrub Wood. Do not climb the stile in the field corner but

Hanningfield Reservoir

turn left to continue along the right-hand field edge and climb a stile on to a lane. Bear left and keep ahead and just before a left bend, turn off right Ⓒ through a gap beside a metal gate and a waymarked post points the way along the right-hand edge of a field. From here there are fine and extensive views to the left, looking across the Thames Estuary to the North Downs.

On entering the next field, pass through a hedge gap, continue downhill along its left edge and pass through another gap. Turn left along the left-hand field edge, and in the corner, turn right and follow the hedge line to the next corner. Turn right along the left-hand field edge and almost immediately bear left through a hedge gap, continue uphill along the right-hand edge of a field and, in the corner, turn right through another hedge gap.

Turn left, keep ahead towards a reservoir embankment, continue below it, beside a high wire fence, and climb a stile on to a lane. Turn right, then turn left Ⓓ over a stile, at a public footpath sign, and walk along the right-hand edge of a field. Continue along a path that bears right to a waymarked post and turn left gently downhill. Ahead is a superb view over Hanningfield Reservoir. In the bottom field corner, follow the path first to the left and then to the right to emerge into the car park of the **Old Windmill** pub. Keep ahead to the road and turn left to retrace your steps to the start.

Chipping Ongar and Greensted church

		GPS waypoints
Start	Chipping Ongar	
Distance	4½ miles (7.4km)	TL 552 031
Height gain	270 feet (80m)	**Ⓐ** TL 550 026
Approximate time	2 hours	**Ⓑ** TL 531 025
Parking	Chipping Ongar	**Ⓒ** TL 528 029
		Ⓓ TL 538 029
Ordnance Survey maps	Landranger 167 (Chelmsford), Explorer 183 (Chelmsford & The Rodings)	

After passing by the moat and earthworks of the largely vanished castle at Chipping Ongar, this well-waymarked route takes you across the gently undulating countryside of the Roding Valley to the famous wooden church at Greensted. From there an easy stroll along the Essex Way leads back to the start.

The walk starts in the centre of the pleasant and ancient market town of Chipping Ongar by the library and Budworth Hall, the latter a Victorian building with a clock tower erected to commemorate Queen Victoria's Golden Jubilee in 1887. Walk through the car park to the left of the library and join a gravel path which passes to the left of an information board and continues beside the castle moat to a kissing-gate. Only the mound or motte remains of the Norman castle.

Go through the kissing-gate, bear right along the right-hand field edge, go through another kissing-gate on to a track and turn right. The track curves left but you bear right along a grassy, fence-lined path to reach a kissing-gate. Go through to emerge on to a lane. A few steps ahead turn right along a walled path and left at the end to pass to the right of the church before reaching the main street. Apart from the 15th-century steeple and 19th-century south aisle and west porch, the church is still basically the original Norman structure built around 1080.

Turn left and, just after crossing a bridge over the River Roding, turn right **Ⓐ** in the Greensted and Toot Hill direction. Later, where the road bends right, keep ahead along a tarmac path, passing the school entrance to a stile. Climb it, walk along the left-hand edge of two fields and then continue along an enclosed path. The path bears left to pass between two pools and on through a belt of trees and bushes to enter a field. Turn right to continue along the right-hand edge, which curves left, and look out for where a waymarked post directs you to turn right through a hedge gap. Turn left, walk along the left-hand edge of two fields separated by a plank footbridge and go through a hedge gap on to a lane **Ⓑ**.

Turn left and after about 20 yards turn right by a public footpath sign on to a path through a belt of trees and continue along the right-hand edge of a field. At a waymarked post, just before

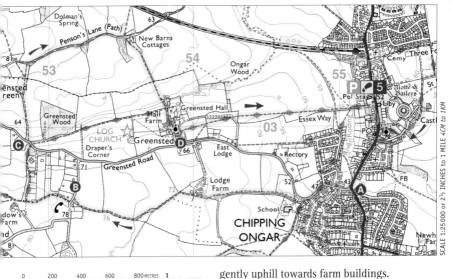

SCALE 1:25 000 or 2½ INCHES to 1 MILE 4CM to 1KM

0	200	400	600	800 METRES	1

KILOMETRES
MILES

0	200	400	600 YARDS	½

reaching a farm, turn right over a stile – here joining the Essex Way – and continue along the left-hand edge of a succession of fields and over a series of stiles. After the last field, keep ahead between trees, bear left to climb a stile and turn right along the right-hand edge of a field, heading gently downhill to a road.

Turn left and, at a public footpath sign to Penson's Lane, turn right **C** over a footbridge and head gently uphill along an enclosed path, by a new plantation on the right. At a waymarked post, pass through a fence gap to a fork and take the right-hand enclosed path. Cross a footbridge and climb a stile, continue along another enclosed path to the right of a field and keep ahead through trees and over a plank footbridge to a T-junction. Turn right and walk along an attractive, tree-lined path (Penson's Lane). After nearly ¼ mile (400m), and just past a footpath post on the left, turn right through trees to enter a field. Bear left along the left-hand field edge, following the edge to the right. Continue gently downhill between fields. At the bottom follow the track around left and right bends and head

gently uphill towards farm buildings. Look out for where a waymark directs you up steps and through a gate and keep ahead along a gravel track to emerge on a lane by Greensted church.

This delightful little Saxon church is of unique interest as the only remaining wooden church in England and indeed it claims to be the oldest wooden church in the world. It was built around 1060, and the wooden walls of the nave survive from the original Saxon structure. Over the centuries the church has been enlarged and restored several times; the chancel was rebuilt in brick around 1500, and the timber tower and shingle spire – complete with traditional Essex weatherboard cladding – probably date from the early 17th century.

Turn left **D** along a tarmac track, at a public footpath sign to Ongar, and where the track bears left, keep ahead through a gate and follow a grassy path across a field to go through a hedge gap in the far left-hand corner. Bear left to continue along the left-hand edge of the next field, go through a kissing-gate, cross a track and keep ahead to cross a plank footbridge.

Keep in a straight line across fields towards Chipping Ongar. Finally cross a bridge over the river and head uphill along a track to the start. ●

Thorndon Country Park

		GPS waypoints	
Start	Thorndon Country Park North, signposted from A128 to south of Brentwood	🔖	TQ 607 914
		A	TQ 614 912
		B	TQ 626 905
Distance	4½ miles (7.4km)	**C**	TQ 617 892
Height gain	400 feet (120m)	**D**	TQ 609 907
Approximate time	2¼ hours		
Parking	Thorndon Country Park North		
Ordnance Survey maps	Landranger 177 (East London), Explorer 175 (Southend-on-Sea & Basildon)		

Thorndon Country Park, a delightful mix of woodland, meadow, heath and pools, was once part of the Thorndon Hall estate, and its winding paths and trails are an opportunity to look for wildlife while offering fine views over the Thames estuary to distant Kent's North Downs. There is a Countryside Centre, which was built from trees uprooted during the 1987 hurricane and has a display area, gift shop and café.

🔖 A track from the south-east corner of the car park heads away, passing left of the Countryside Centre. However, before getting there, almost immediately leave left onto another broad track between the trees. Approaching a bench, turn right as indicated by an 'ALL' paths waypost. Keep going, passing a second 'ALL' paths waypost and then crossing a wooden bridge. Reaching a junction by a bench, go left. Before long the path swings sharply right in front of a couple

In Thorndon Country Park

of gates. Reaching a T-junction, go left, walking beside a fenced area. Carry on to meet a drive at Whittington Bars Gate **A**.

Cross to the continuing trail opposite. Walk on, ignoring subsequent side paths, eventually breaking from the trees to continue at the edge of grassland. Towards the far end, watch for a waymark and bear off left along a narrower path into the trees.

Arriving at a crossing path in front of the Menagerie Plantation **B**, go right. After passing through a gate, immediately turn off left along a grass ride through open woodland. Keep ahead at a junction, later passing a seat. The way then narrows, soon gently descending to a T-junction at the bottom. Go right and then wind left over a ditch, rising beyond to continue past Old Hall Pond.

At the far end of the lake turn right and leave the wood through a gate.

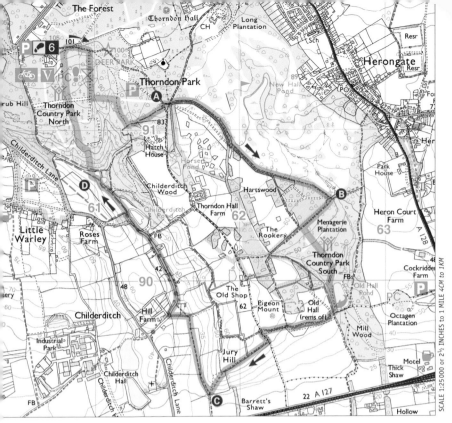

SCALE 1:25000 or 2½ INCHES to 1 MILE 4CM to 1KM

0	200	400	600	800 METRES	1
					KILOMETRES
					MILES
0	200	400	600 YARDS	½	

Walking forward, join a gravel track and follow it left at the edge of open grassland. Over to the right, trees conceal the site of the Old Hall, while the Pigeon Mount a little further on is where a dovecote-summerhouse once stood. Immediately through a gateway near an information board, turn left off the track and follow a grass swathe down beside the hedge. Swing within the corner along the bottom edge, later passing through another gap to continue in the next meadow. Reaching the corner, drop left through a gate and bear right, heading downhill towards scrub where there is a gate at the bottom **C**.

However, rather than go through, swing sharp right in front of the gate on a rising path beside an outgrown hedge. Through a gate at the end, follow a trod across a long field, closing with its left edge to the far left corner. Over a foot-bridge, keep going by a fence. Ignoring a gate at the end, swing left to follow a track out to a lane near Hill Farm.

Go right. At the end of the lane, keep ahead on a woodland path. Bear left where it soon forks and keep ahead at a second junction, a little further on. The path rises past a small pond before emerging into the corner of rough grassland. Walk on along the bottom edge, passing a metal double gate seen over to the right. After walking through a small area of scrub, look right for a wooden bridle gate **D** leaving into the trees.

Cross a bridge over a ditch to a junction and take the path ahead, waymarked to the café, which climbs into the wood. Reaching a T-junction, go left, but as the trail then crests, fork off right. Ignore a couple of crossing paths, and carry on back to the Countryside Centre and car park. ●

Cymbeline Meadows and Colchester

		GPS waypoints
Start	Cymbeline Meadows Farm Trail, signposted from the A133 (Colchester bypass) where Spring Lane meets Bakers Lane	🖉 TL 975 259 Ⓐ TL 984 259 Ⓑ TL 997 252 Ⓒ TL 997 256 Ⓓ TL 991 257
Distance	4½ miles (7.2km)	
Height gain	220 feet (65m)	
Approximate time	2 hours	
Parking	By the trail entrance, in The Chase Way	
Ordnance Survey maps	Landranger 168 (Colchester), Explorer 184 (Colchester)	

Much of this attractive walk is beside the lovely River Colne and Cymbeline Meadows, an area of water meadows, picnic spots and controlled grazing, offering a peaceful approach to Colchester, the oldest recorded town in Britain. There is only one stretch of the walk along a short underpass – the rest is through meadows, along riverside paths and through the lovely Castle Park. Be sure to allow plenty of time to explore the many sites in the centre of this historic Roman town.

🖉 Start by the Cymbeline Meadows Farm Trail information board. The raised Iron Age earth bank behind you, known as Lexden Dyke, was constructed by hand as a defence more than 2,000 years ago.

Take the gravel footpath ahead, signposted Sheepen Road, go through a kissing-gate and follow the riverside path, to the left of the River Colne, past a footbridge. In the distance you'll notice the Victorian water tower, known locally as 'Jumbo'. Go through another kissing-gate and as the river curves right, keep ahead along the left-hand edge of the next two fields, passing through a kissing-gate in between them. At the end of the second field go through a kissing-gate and turn right to cross a footbridge Ⓐ (Sheepen Bridge).

Follow the enclosed path to go though a kissing-gate to a road (Cymbeline Way). Turn left, cross this busy road and keep ahead along Sheepen Road, looking out for where you turn right opposite a school, in the Lexden direction.

Take the enclosed public footpath to the right of a cycle path. Cross a track to the entrance to Hilly Fields Nature Reserve and keep ahead along the path as it later passes to the right of Colchester Institute.

At a junction of paths, keep ahead as the undulating path crosses a field and heads uphill to pass beside a barrier to a junction. Cross to Popes Lane opposite, keeping ahead at the end over a

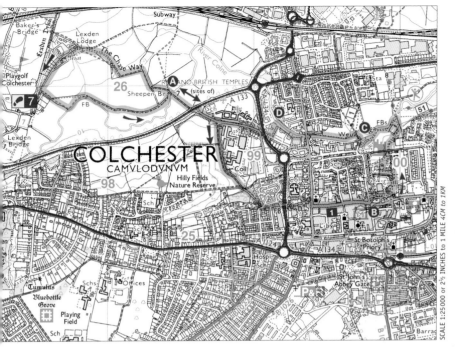

footbridge spanning the dual carriageway to reach Balkerne Gate.

This well-preserved entrance was built in AD 50 to mark the foundation of the walled town of Colchester and was one of the largest gateways in Roman Britain. The walls on either side of it are Britain's oldest.

Wind right and left around the **Hole in the Wall** pub, and keep ahead past the Mercury Theatre and the 'Jumbo' water tower. Follow the street as it winds left and right to a junction opposite St Peter's Church. Turn right to traffic lights, there crossing left to walk along High Street. The area behind the George Hotel was part of Colchester's Dutch Quarter, so called because Dutch refugees settled in this part of the town in the 16th and 17th centuries.

After ¼ mile (400m), turn left along Museum Street **B** which leads to Colchester Castle. With its well-preserved stretches of Roman walls, Norman castle, ruins of St Botolph's Priory, Dutch Quarter and narrow

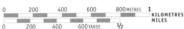

streets lined by attractive old buildings, Colchester is one of the most interesting and historic towns in the country and merits a lengthy exploration. It was an important tribal capital – Camulodunum – long before the Romans arrived and made it one of the principal cities of Roman Britain. Over 1,000 years later in AD 1076, William the Conqueror began construction on this impressive castle, the largest Norman keep in Europe. It was built on the site of a Roman temple, using recycled bricks and stones from the ruined Roman city. The castle now houses an excellent museum, which includes many Roman artefacts.

Pass to the right of the castle keep and bear left at Hollytrees Museum. Go through a gap in a wall to continue on a downhill path through this beautiful park, passing a **café** to a T-junction. Turn right to go through gates in the Roman walls and carry on ahead, passing the thatched bowls club to reach a riverside path. Go left beside the River Colne.

Keeping right of a boating lake, leave Colchester Castle Park through the gates and immediately turn right to cross a footbridge ⓒ beside Middle Mill Weir, once the site of an 11th century mill. Turn left, now with the river on your left and continue along this riverside path to climb steps to a road beside a row of timbered cottages. Cross the bridge and then leave right through a gap at the end of railings to double back to the river. Carry on upstream, the path shortly approaching a mini-roundabout ⓓ. Turn off left just before it, past apartments and a parking area to a street at the far side. Cross and bear right through an underpass to reach the other side of a dual carriageway.

Turn right and ascend the ramp and bear left along Sheepen Road. After 300 yards you will rejoin the route back across Cymbeline Way following the enclosed path to recross Sheepen Bridge ⓐ.

Keep ahead along a gravel path and bear left at a Colne Valley waymarked fingerpost. Bear right at the next fingerpost to pass to the right of a farmhouse cottage.

At a meeting of paths turn left along a concrete track by a waymarked post and keep ahead as the path becomes a gravel lane and winds back to the start. ●

Colchester Castle

Finchingfield and Great Bardfield

Start	Finchingfield	**GPS waypoints**	
Distance	4½ miles (7.3km)	✎ TL 684 327	
Height gain	220 feet (65m)	Ⓐ TL 669 318	
		Ⓑ TL 673 306	
Approximate time	2 hours	Ⓒ TL 677 305	
Parking	Around The Green at Finchingfield	Ⓓ TL 686 327	
Ordnance Survey maps	Landranger 167 (Chelmsford), Explorer 195 (Braintree & Saffron Walden)		

There are plenty of wide and extensive views, two beautiful villages and two fine medieval churches on this walk. From the picture postcard village of Finchingfield, the route heads across fields and by the little River Pant to the almost equally attractive village of Great Bardfield. The return leg is mostly alongside Finchingfield Brook. Expect to encounter some muddy and overgrown paths in places.

Finchingfield has often been described as the prettiest village in Essex and it is easy to see why. A spacious green, lined by attractive old cottages, overlooks a duck pond and beyond the road climbs gently to the 13th- to 14th-century church. This picturesque scene is further enhanced by the 18th-century cupola on the Norman tower of the church. Pubs and cafés cater for the many visitors.

✎ With your back to the war memorial and facing the pond, follow the road right beside the green. As it bends at the end, take the last of three drives coming together on the right. Marked as a footpath, it climbs away past houses. Keep ahead where it then bends, following an enclosed path behind more houses which comes out into the corner of a large field.

Keep ahead on a grassy path, which, partway along, moves across the ditch to run at the edge of the adjacent field. Wind left within the corner and

then right to meet the corner of a gravel track. Follow it ahead towards a copse, winding left and then right to continue beyond at the edge of a couple of fields. Curve right across a final field to come out onto a lane by Beslyns Cottage Ⓐ.

Follow it left, keeping ahead at a junction. Where the lane subsequently bends left, leave over a stile on the right into the corner of paddocks. Head down by the left hedge towards trees, where, just before the bottom, there is a stile on the left. A path leads away beside the River Pant, shortly passing a gauging station. Over another stile, carry on along the field beyond, curving with the river to a gate at the far end near farm buildings. Just beyond, turn right over a bridge.

Just beyond, turn right over a footbridge spanning the river and then go left along the field edge above the opposite bank. Further on, just after the

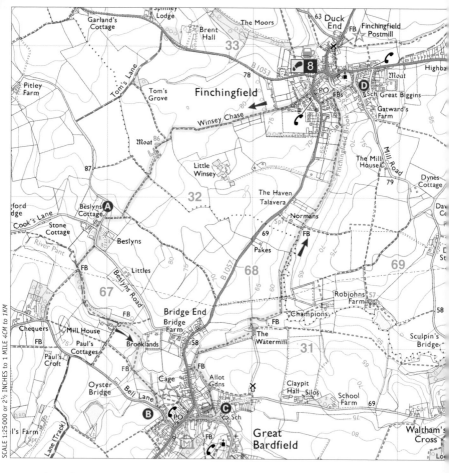

SCALE 1:25000 or 2½ INCHES to 1 MILE 4CM to 1KM

field boundary swings right, the path moves left to continue with the hedge then on your right. Carry on at the edge of a small plantation, a path then joining from the right. Cross a bridged ditch and carry on through unkempt scrub to a fork. Bear right, soon emerging onto Bell Lane **B**.

Head left into Great Bardfield. At the end, go left again through the village. Approaching a small green on which stands the war memorial cross, bear right and walk down to a second green. Keep left but then, immediately after crossing a small stream, turn off left across grass to find a footpath leaving in the corner **C**. It runs beside the stream behind houses, eventually leading out to the edge of a field.

Go left, following the brook into a shallow corner. Over a stile, turn right along the edge of the next field and walk on, shortly joining a track that leads into the yard of the old Watermill. Bear left through the yard to cross the mill stream by the house, a grass trod leading on to a second bridge over the main river into a field.

Turn right along the boundary, swinging within the corner to meet a crossing track. Go right through the hedge and then immediately left along an enclosed path beside paddocks. The path soon crosses to run along the other flank before emerging to the edge of a field. Go right but then swing left within the corner to carry on at the field edge. Keep going in the fields beyond beside Finchingfield Brook, watching for the path moving behind the fence. Eventually, the path opens to wind through trees and then behind house gardens to meet a crossing tarmac path. Follow it right across the stream to emerge onto a narrow lane. Turn right behind the churchyard to meet another lane **D** and go left. Reaching the main road, turn left again to return to the village green and pond. ●

Finchingfield

Mersea Island

		GPS waypoints
Start	Cudmore Grove Country Park, signposted from B1025 immediately after crossing to Mersea Island	🖉 TM 065 146 🅐 TM 069 147 🅑 TM 062 152 🅒 TM 044 143 🅓 TM 051 135
Distance	5½ miles (8.9km)	
Height gain	120 feet (35m)	
Approximate time	2½ hours	
Parking	Cudmore Grove Country Park	
Ordnance Survey maps	Landranger 168 (Colchester), Explorer 184 (Colchester)	

Mersea Island lies just off the Essex coast amid the estuaries of the Blackwater and Colne. The first and last parts of the route are along the coast at the eastern tip of the island; the middle stretch is across meadowland, passing the old church at East Mersea. This is a walk of wide and extensive views, looking across the flat expanses of the island and the surrounding waters to the mainland.

A mixture of meadows, marshland and low cliffs make up Cudmore Grove Country Park. Between the two World Wars the area was a golf course, it later became a Second World War defence site, then farmland and in 1974 was bought by Essex County Council as a place of public enjoyment and recreation.

🖉 At a sign 'Beach', head across grass to join a track and, passing to the left of a wartime pillbox, follow the track to the shore and turn left on to the sea wall 🅐. Ahead are views of Brightlingsea on the other side of the Colne Estuary. Continue along the sea wall. The path later swings left and, after just over 100 yards, bear left to descend the embankment, cross a channel and walk along an enclosed path, passing to the left of a house. Keep ahead along a track to a lane, continue to where the lane bends left 🅑 and keep ahead along a track to a stile. Climb it, walk along a

narrow path parallel to the track and climb three stiles to enter a meadow.

Continue along the left-hand edge of the meadow and, at the corner of the wire fence on the left, keep straight ahead to a stile and fence corner. Do not climb the stile but turn right across the meadow, making for the corner of trees, where you turn left over a stile to continue along an attractive, tree-lined track. Where this track bends left, keep ahead, go through a kissing-gate and continue along the left-hand edge of a meadow. At a waymarked post, keep straight ahead to the next one and then continue alongside a hedge on the right to the corner of the meadow.

Keep ahead through a kissing-gate and walk along the right-hand edge of a succession of fields, passing through a series of hedge gaps.

Later follow the field edge as it curves first left and then right and finally walk

Mersea Island

along a short section of enclosed track to a narrow lane. Turn left to a T-junction **C**, turn left along the road into the hamlet of East Mersea and turn right down Church Lane to the medieval church, thought to stand on the site of a Viking camp.

Continue past the church along a tarmac drive through a holiday park, pass beside a gate and keep ahead along a hedge-lined track, which bears left to reach a section of new sea wall **D**. Turn left along it, passing in front of a beach **café** and chalets and, after the wall ends, continue by the shore across a mixture of grass, sand and stones. Later continue along the beach below low cliffs – *the clifftop path is not a right of way and is also dangerous because of the crumbly nature of the cliffs* – to regain the sea wall near the start of the walk **A**. Immediately turn left to return to the car park. ●

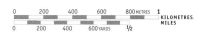

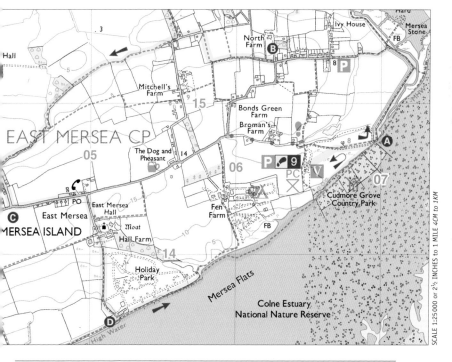

Weald Country Park

		GPS waypoints	
Start	Weald Country Park, Visitor Centre car park, follow signs to South Weald	🖋	TQ 568 941
		Ⓐ	TQ 571 945
Distance	5 miles (8.2km)	Ⓑ	TQ 567 964
Height gain	400 feet (120m)	Ⓒ	TQ 573 959
Approximate time	2½ hours	Ⓓ	TQ 577 948
Parking	Weald Country Park	Ⓔ	TQ 572 940
Ordnance Survey maps	Landranger 167 (Chelmsford), Explorer 175 (Southend-on-Sea & Basildon)		

Lakes, woodland and grassland combine to create an attractive and satisfying walk in the Weald Country Park just to the north-west of Brentwood. There are fine views over the parkland, and in spring the woods are carpeted with bluebells. The route extends slightly northwards beyond the park to Bentley Common and also includes South Weald village.

In the Middle Ages, Weald Country Park was part of a hunting ground, used by both medieval monarchs and the abbots of Waltham. It comprises a mixture of woodland and grassland and has two lakes, plus several ponds.

🖋 Start at the visitor centre and in the far corner of the car park – by a Country Park noticeboard – take the tree-lined track which heads downhill to the lake. Cross a causeway between two lakes, turn right over a bridge and walk along a pleasant wooded path beside the lake. At the end of the lake, bear left across grass into woodland and turn left along a track Ⓐ.

Head steadily uphill, keeping close to the left-hand, inside edge of the trees, later continuing first through a belt of woodland and then along a hedge-lined track to pass beside a barrier and later a stile. Climb it, keep ahead to a road, cross over, walk along the tarmac drive opposite and then continue through a kissing-gate.

Continue across a field and, at a hedge corner, climb a stile and keep straight ahead across the next field, and bear slightly left across the third one to another stile. Climb that, then turn right along the right-hand field edge, climb a stile, continue along the left-hand edge of the next field and climb a stile on to a track Ⓑ.

St Paul's Church at Bentley Common is to the left but the route continues to the right along the tree-lined track called Pilgrim's Lane. It may well be muddy. In the Middle Ages this was a route taken by pilgrims on their way to Canterbury. On emerging on to a lane, turn right Ⓒ to a road, cross over and keep ahead along the tarmac drive to the Civic Amenity and Recycling Centre. Just before the gates to the centre, bear right beside a barrier and bear right again along a path which curves left.

Follow this winding path into woodland to a T-junction, turn left and after

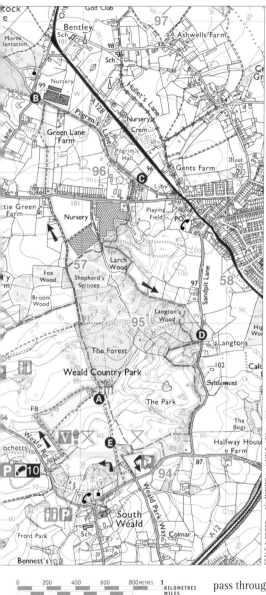

stile on to a track **D**. Turn right and just where the field to your left ends turn left along a path through trees and head down to a gate.

Go through, turn left and keep along another undulating path, which winds along the left-hand edge of grassland, in and out of trees, curving right just before reaching a barrier. The path continues along the edge of the park, bending right again to keep parallel to a road and later bearing right away from the road. At a fork – just before reaching two fairly close waymarked posts – take the right-hand path across grass (do not turn left to a road), which later keeps to the right of a cricket field to reach a gate. Go through, continue along an enclosed path, which turns left and then turn right to join a track and keep ahead to a Country Park noticeboard **E**.

For a brief detour into South Weald, turn left, walk across the grass to pass through a fence and turn right on to a path above the road to the church and pub. South Weald church was mainly rebuilt in the 19th century but retains its fine medieval tower. Return to the Country Park noticeboard and keep ahead through the fence gap beside it. Bear left, in the direction of the visitor centre, to head across grass to the start, enjoying the grand views to the right across the park, with the lake below and woodland on the horizon. ●

a few yards turn left again at a blue-waymarked post and follow the path ahead. The rest of the route follows blue 'Horseride' waymarks through the Country Park. Continue through mixed woodland, turning right along the left-hand edge of the trees to a T-junction. Turn left and keep along a winding and undulating path to eventually climb a

SCALE 1:25 000 or 2½ INCHES to 1 MILE 4CM to 1KM

0   200   400   600   800 METRES   1
0   200   400   600 YARDS   ½
KILOMETRES
MILES

Pleshey and Great Waltham

		GPS waypoints
Start	Pleshey	⬛ TL 663 143
Distance	5½ miles (8.9km)	Ⓐ TL 664 135
Height gain	170 feet (50m)	Ⓑ TL 684 134
Approximate time	2½ hours	Ⓒ TL 695 136
Parking	Roadside parking at Pleshey	Ⓓ TL 689 140
Ordnance Survey maps	Landranger 167 (Chelmsford), Explorer 183 (Chelmsford & The Rodings)	Ⓔ TL 667 146

The outward route is along the south side of the valley of Walthambury Brook between Pleshey and Great Waltham. The return follows the well-waymarked Essex Way along the north side, keeping by the brook for much of the way. There are fine views across the valley, and on the final part of the route you walk beside the medieval earthworks that enclose the village of Pleshey.

Pleshey is a most attractive and interesting village with a sloping main street lined by old cottages – some of them thatched – the moat and earthworks of a Norman castle, and a handsome, mainly Victorian church, built on the site of its medieval predecessor. In addition the whole village is enclosed by a defensive earthwork, probably constructed around the same time as the castle, which is followed on the last leg of the route.

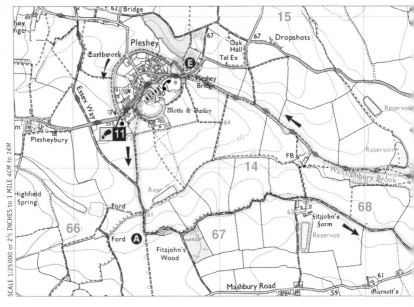

🖉 With your back to the church, head right towards the village centre. After 100 yards, turn off right down Pump Lane. Just beyond the houses, there is a glimpse of the castle mound (open only by prior appointment) through a gate on the left. The route, however, leaves to the right along an enclosed path between paddocks, emerging through a gap at the end onto the bend of a concrete farm track. Follow it ahead, later dipping by a pond over to the left and rising beyond to a junction **Ⓐ**.

Leave left along a gravel track marked as a bridleway. Shortly reaching a fork, take the left branch. Wind on for another ¾ mile (1.2km) to Fitzjohn's Farm. At a junction there, go right and then immediately left to continue with the track. It eventually ends at a lane **Ⓑ**.

Turn left, passing High Houses. Keep with the main lane as it bends right in front of a junction and carry on to the end of the lane by the **Beehive** pub in front of the church at Great Waltham.

It is thought that the village church was founded in the 11th century by Geoffrey de Mandeville of Pleshey Castle. It is noted for an unusually wide Norman nave and fine 16th century roof. The lime walk beside the church emerges beside the impressive Guild Hall, which originates in a 14th-century cottage. Its present Elizabethan form dates from the late 16th century.

Turn left in front of the church, walking down the hill and leaving the village over a bridge across Walthambury Brook. Walk on a little further to find a path signed off through the hedge on the left **Ⓒ**, immediately before the bus stop. Walk away at the edge of a large field, coming out onto another lane at the far side **Ⓓ**. Cross to a track opposite by cottages at Walthambury Farm, which winds away left and then right, skirting below the banks of a small reservoir. Reaching a T-junction with a farm track, turn left. Walk on at the field edge, later approaching the corner of another reservoir. The path dips left in front of the bank, swinging left again at the far side across the field towards woodland. Approaching the trees, turn right in front of a concrete field access bridge and continue at the field edge above Walthambury Brook.

Walk on at the edge of successive fields, eventually crossing a small footbridge over a side ditch. Shortly after, in the corner of the field by a waypost, fork left over a footbridge spanning the brook, and bear right to continue above its other bank. Towards the far end of the field, the way becomes contained before finally coming out onto a lane **Ⓔ**.

Cross to another footpath opposite, keeping left as it almost immediately forks. The obvious path curves through trees to emerge at the edge of a field. Go left, quickly swinging right alongside the medieval village boundary ditch. Reaching another lane, cross to the ongoing path opposite. Over a footbridge, keep going at the edge of a second field to come out opposite the church. ●

Hatfield Forest

		GPS waypoints
Start	Hatfield Forest, National Trust car park on lane signposted to Bush End and Hatfield Forest from A120 at Takeley	🖉 TL 547 202 **A** TL 547 199 **B** TL 556 210 **C** TL 533 212 **D** TL 540 198
Distance	5½ miles (8.9km)	
Height gain	170 feet (50m)	
Approximate time	2½ hours	
Parking	Hatfield Forest	
Ordnance Survey maps	Landranger 167 (Chelmsford), Explorers 183 (Chelmsford & The Rodings) and 195 (Braintree & Saffron Walden)	

The first part of this flat and easy walk is across fields to join the Flitch Way, a disused railway track. You then follow the tree-lined way along the edge of Hatfield Forest before entering it. The remainder of the route is across the grassy plains, by the lake and through the woodlands of the forest, one of the finest and least altered survivals of the medieval Forest of Essex. Do not let the sound and sight at times of planes landing and taking off from nearby Stansted Airport put you off what is a most attractive and satisfying walk.

Along with Epping and Hainault, Hatfield Forest is one of the surviving remnants of the Forest of Essex, a vast royal hunting ground which in the Middle Ages extended over much of the county. As a result of careful and traditional methods of management over the centuries, it is little changed and probably resembles a medieval forested area more closely than anywhere else in the country. In 1729 the forest was acquired by the Houblon family, who were responsible for the lake and Shell House. It is now managed by the National Trust and because of its unique landscape value it has been designated a National Nature Reserve.

🖉 Begin by leaving the car park and turning right along the lane, passing a tiny church. Turn left along the lane signposted to Bush End **A** and, where it bears right, turn left over a stile and take the path ahead across a field. Climb a stile on the far side, walk along the left-hand edge of a field to a T-junction and turn left on to a track, which bends right to continue along the right-hand edge of a field. Where the track turns left, keep ahead along a path to continue by field edges and, in the corner of the last field, turn right and then immediately left through a hedge gap on to a straight, tree-lined path **B**.

This is the Flitch Way, a footpath, cycle and bridleway created from the former Braintree to Bishop's Stortford Railway. After crossing a bridge over a lane, the path continues along the right-hand edge of Hatfield Forest.

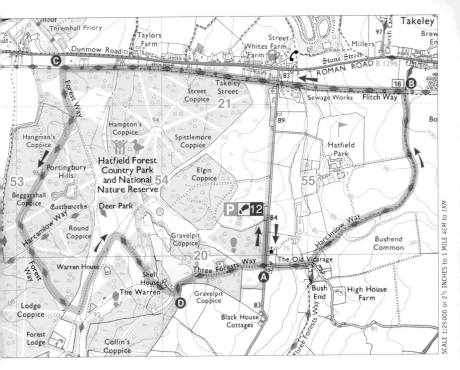

After 1 mile (1.6km), at a Forest Way post **C**, turn left and go through a gate. Joining the Forest Way to enter the woods, keep ahead along a faint grassy path across an open area. At the second Forest Way fingerpost follow the direction of the yellow waymark and turn right. Keep ahead at a crossroads (by the corner of a wire fence on the left) and the path bears left to another crossroads.

Keep ahead to eventually emerge into a large open area and bear left across it to meet a stony track. Turn left along this curving track to a T-junction and turn right along a tarmac drive to a car park and National Trust information board by a junction of tracks and paths. Turn left through a gate and take the path that passes in front of the **café** and Shell House. The latter, an 18th-century picnic room, is so called because it is decorated with shells and flints.

Bear left **D** to continue across the end of the lake and, immediately on entering woodland, turn right through trees to a stile. Climb it. Keep ahead to climb another stile on to a lane **A**. Turn left to return to the starting point. ●

In Hatfield Forest

St Osyth Creek

		GPS waypoints	
Start	St Osyth		TM 121 155
Distance	6¼ miles (10km)	**A**	TM 114 152
Height gain	155 feet (45m)	**B**	TM 083 157
Approximate time	3 hours	**C**	TM 094 149
Parking	St Osyth, by Priory Gatehouse	**D**	TM 113 149
Ordnance Survey maps	Landranger 168 (Colchester), Explorer 184 (Colchester)		

There are wide and extensive views across meadows, creeks and marshes as you walk along the path beside St Osyth and later Brightlingsea creeks to the martello tower near Point Clear. This is followed by nearly 1¹/₂ miles of quiet road walking. A final stretch across fields and by the end of Mill Dam Lake leads back to the start. An alternative route, retracing your steps along the creekside path, is provided for those who prefer to avoid the road walking.

The small village of St Osyth is dominated by its priory, founded in the early 12th century as a house of Augustinian canons. After its dissolution in 1539, a large house was built on the site, incorporating many of the monastic structures, and this was subsequently extended both in the 18th and 19th

centuries. The 15th-century gatehouse – where the walk begins – is considered one of the finest in the country and is the main survival of the medieval monastery. Almost opposite is the mainly Tudor parish church.

Facing the priory gatehouse, turn left along the road, which bears left to

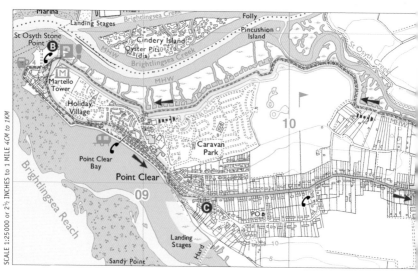

St Osyth Creek

cross a bridge over the end of Mill Dam Lake. On the other side, turn right **Ⓐ** at a public footpath sign, along a path that keeps along the edge of the marshes beside St Osyth Creek. Follow this winding path – mainly along the top of an embankment and through several kissing-gates – for almost 2¹⁄₂ miles (4km). Towards the end you pass beside a large caravan park on the left and to the right the views are dominated by the docks at Brightlingsea.

Eventually the path curves left

around St Osyth Stone Point and continues – now concreted – in front of chalets and bungalows. When you see a martello tower on the left, turn left **Ⓑ** off the coast path and walk along a track, passing to the left of both the **Ferry Inn** and the martello tower. The latter is now an aviation and 1940s museum.

*At this point, those who wish to avoid about 1¹⁄₂ (2.4km) miles of road walking can retrace their steps to the bridge over the end of Mill Dam Lake **Ⓐ**. Turn right along the road and rejoin the main route by turning left along a narrow lane where the road bends right **Ⓓ**.*

For the main walk, continue along the track through part of the caravan park and between houses to a road at Point Clear. Keep ahead to a junction, bear right along a tarmac drive (Sea View Terrace) and continue along a gently ascending path above a beach. The path bears gradually left to rejoin the road **Ⓒ** and you keep along it to where it bends to the left **Ⓓ** (Wigboro Wick Lane).

Bear right here along a narrow lane. Across the fields to the left, the houses, church and priory gatehouse at St Osyth can be seen slightly elevated above the surrounding countryside. Where the lane bends right, keep ahead to a public footpath sign then along a track across fields. Just before reaching the corner of a field, turn left on to a track, which heads towards St Osyth. Descend to cross a bridge over the end of Mill Dam Lake, ascend to a farm and continue between farm buildings to emerge on to the road opposite the start. ●

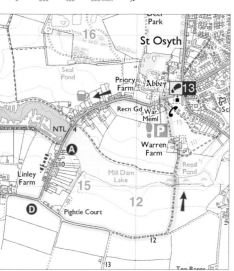

Through the Colne Valley

		GPS waypoints
Start	Earls Colne High Street	
Distance	5 miles (8km)	📷 TL 857 289
Height gain	325 feet (100m)	**A** TL 854 300
		B TL 852 309
Approximate time	2½ hours	**C** TL 841 312
Parking	In car park behind the Co-op, Queen's Road	**D** TL 847 301
Ordnance Survey maps	Landranger 167 (Chelmsford), Explorer 195 (Braintree & Saffron Walden)	

This lovely, varied walk captures the essence of the beautiful Colne Valley and includes woodland, the meandering River Colne, quiet lanes and two pretty villages. Both churches on this walk share the same name and their towers bear the coat of arms and heraldic symbol of the five-pointed star of the Earls of Oxford otherwise known as the de Vere family. John de Vere, who inherited his title from a distant cousin, completed the church tower in Earls Colne in 1534.

More recently, in the 19th century, the Hunt family left their mark on Earls Colne and developed Atlas Works, a company, which made agricultural machinery. To make transport easier the Colne Valley Railway was opened in 1860 and many new homes were built to house workers. The business and railway have long since closed but their legacy remains and is documented in a local museum, situated in a water tower near to the original workshops.

📷 Start in Earls Colne High Street facing the library and notice the plaque 'Hunt' above the door. Turn right and right again at **The Lion** pub into Burrows Road. Cross the road ahead (Hillie Bunnies) and continue to a stile. Climb it and keep ahead along an enclosed path to join a wide grassy path that crosses Earls Colne Golf Course. Continue downhill – *looking out for low flying golf balls* – and pass to the left of a pond, and shortly afterwards, cross a footbridge over the River Colne. Bear slightly left and continue ahead to pass through a hedge gap, (to the right is the disused railway trackbed now a nature walk), and turn left to reach a waymarked post just before a weir. Turn right here to continue uphill along an enclosed track towards Lodge Farm. Pass beside a metal gate and turn left (Mill Lane). From here are fine views over the Colne Valley.

After 200 yards leave right at a public bridleway sign **A** and continue along the right edge of a field. The spire of the 12th century St Andrew's Church in Colne Engaine can be seen to the left.

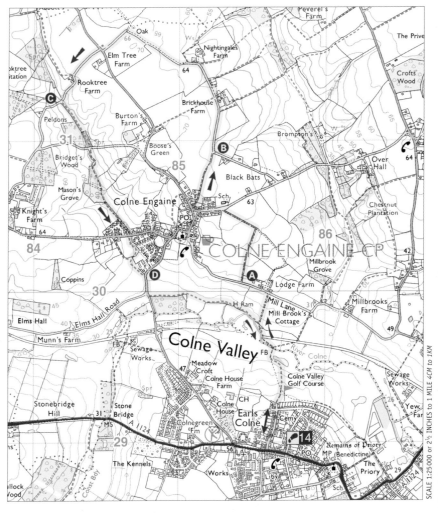

SCALE 1:25000 or 2½ INCHES to 1 MILE 4CM to 1KM

```
0    200    400    600    800 METRES  1
                                        KILOMETRES
                                        MILES
0    200    400    600 YARDS    ½
```

Pass through a hedge gap and then along the left edge of the next field and at the corner turn left to reach a road. Turn left again at Colne Engaine's triangular village green. Keep along the right-hand edge to turn right in between two houses by a public footpath sign, along another enclosed path which leads into a field. Keep ahead along the left field edge to a lane **B**.

Bear left along this quiet country lane that passes three farms and later skirts open fields. Continue ahead at the

crossroads, signposted Buntings Green, along a narrow lane that passes a farm-house and continues downhill. Before it ascends, turn left at a public footpath sign **C** along the right edge of a field, which later veers right to enter woodland.

Pass a fingerpost and cross a footbridge and continue as the path runs beside a brook. Listen out for woodpeckers and owls here. Cross a lane and keep ahead along the right edge of a field. At a waymarked post turn right into this tranquil woodland. Follow the path, now to the right of the brook, as it meanders through the trees, later passing a waymarked post and a row of houses to emerge onto a road. Cross it, go over the stile opposite by a public footpath sign and follow, initially the left edge of a field, then keep ahead to a hedge gap. Head diagonally across the next field to the right of farm buildings to a waymarked post and turn left along the left edge of the next field. Leave left through a hedge gap to a road **D**.

Turn right and just past a triangular green turn left at a public footpath sign, to cross a footbridge into a field. Bear right and follow the field edge round to the left of a wood. Cross a field and go through a hedge gap to enter a 'conservation walks' area. Continue along the left edge of the next field and pass through another hedge gap. Keep ahead to go through another hedge gap, and follow the right edge of the next field, beside the River Colne. Just past Earls Colne River Gauging Station, rejoin the outward walk and retrace your steps to the start. Continue ahead along the High Street to visit St Andrew's Church.

●

Colne Valley

Thaxted

		GPS waypoints
Start	Thaxted	
Distance	6 miles (9.6km)	TL 611 309
Height gain	335 feet (100m)	**A** TL 609 310
Approximate time	3 hours	**B** TL 587 314
		C TL 593 306
Parking	Thaxted	**D** TL 607 300
Ordnance Survey maps	Landranger 167 (Chelmsford), Explorer 195 (Braintree & Saffron Walden)	

This walk takes you through the pleasant, gently rolling countryside of the Chelmer Valley to the north, west and south of Thaxted. For part of the way the tower and spire of Thaxted church and the nearby windmill serve as landmarks. Be prepared for some of the narrow paths to be muddy after rain and overgrown during the summer. It is worthwhile allowing time for an exploration of Thaxted, a particularly attractive small town.

One of the largest and finest parish churches in the country rises above Thaxted and the surrounding countryside. The reason why a small town should boast such a magnificent church is that in the later Middle Ages Thaxted thrived as a centre for both the cutlery and woollen industries. The church was rebuilt on its present lofty and spacious lines in the 14th century and has a tower and spire 181 feet (55m) high.

The superb, timber-framed, 15th-century Guildhall below the church and other fine buildings in the town centre also reflect Thaxted's medieval prosperity. A plaque on the wall of a house in Town Street records that it was the home of the composer Gustav Holst, and it is thought that he wrote part of the *Planets Suite* while there.

The walk starts in front of the Guildhall. Walk up the main street to the right of it, passing the church, to the Bull Ring and just after the main road bends right, turn left **A** along a lane signed 'Watling Street, Cul de Sac'. The lane bends right, at a fork take the left-hand lane, heading downhill. The lane narrows to a track and crosses the infant River Chelmer. Where it turns right to a house, keep ahead along a track, which bends left and continues along the right-hand edge of a field.

The route then continues along a narrow, enclosed path. Emerging from this, turn right and walk across a field and pass through a hedge gap on the far side. Continue along the left-hand edge of a young plantation, then along an enclosed path. Go through another hedge gap and keep ahead to a T-junction. Turn left along a track, passing to the left of a barn, and the track becomes enclosed. At the end of the enclosed section, keep ahead along a concrete track, bear left on joining another one and follow it to a road **B**.

Turn left. After 100 yards, at a public

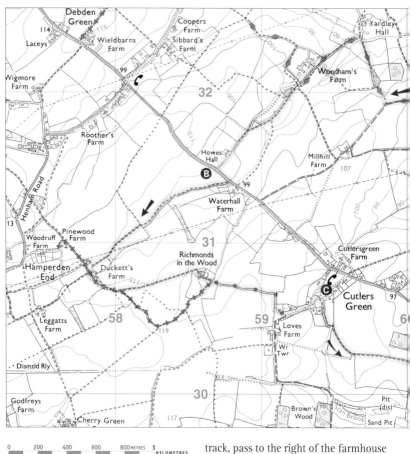

Scale bar:
```
0    200    400    600    800 METRES   1
                                       KILOMETRES
                                       MILES
0    200    400    600 YARDS   ½
```

footpath sign, turn right and walk along the left-hand edge of fields. Keep ahead through a hedge gap, cross a plank footbridge, climb a stile and continue along the right-hand edge of the next field. In the corner, turn right over a stile, and turn left along the left-hand field edge. In the corner, go right to continue along the left-hand edge of the next field. Just beyond the corner of a high wire fence, turn left to a track. Turn left along it, passing a farm. Where the track turns right into a field, keep ahead along an enclosed, tree-lined path.

On emerging into a field, keep along its left-hand edge. The path then continues between fields towards a farm. At a waymarked post to the left of the farm buildings, turn right on to a track, pass to the right of the farmhouse and continue along a drive, which bends first right and then curves left to a T-junction. Turn left along a narrow lane. After 250 yards, at a public footpath sign, turn right **C** on to a path, which becomes enclosed and continues through a belt of woodland to emerge into a field.

Turn left along another short enclosed stretch and then bear right to walk along a left-hand field edge. Go through a hedge gap, turn left to pass through another gap and follow a wide grassy track along the left-hand edge of a field. After going through another hedge gap bear left and head gently downhill along the left-hand edge of the next two fields and over to the left is a fine view of Thaxted church and windmill. In the bottom corner, keep ahead along an enclosed track, do not

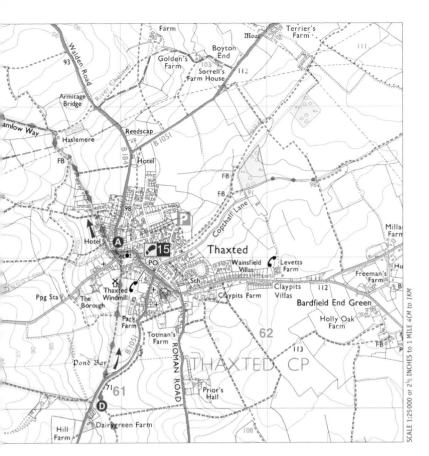

join a tarmac drive but continue along the enclosed track that keeps parallel to the drive, eventually emerging on to it and continuing down to a road **D**.

Turn left and where the road curves slightly right – just before the gate to a house – turn left through a hedge gap. Walk along a path that passes to the left of the house and heads gently uphill along the right-hand field edge directly towards the windmill and church. The windmill was built in 1804 by John Webb, a local farmer, on the site of an earlier one.

Pass to the right of the windmill to join an enclosed tarmac path and go through a kissing-gate. Take the left fork in front of a row of cottages, go through another kissing-gate and continue between cottages and in front of the church to a road. Turn right downhill to the start.

Thaxted church

Castle Hedingham and the River Colne

Castle Hedingham
and the River Colne

		GPS waypoints
Start	Castle Hedingham	📝 TL 785 355
Distance	6 miles (9.7km)	Ⓐ TL 784 358
Height gain	415 feet (125m)	Ⓑ TL 788 355
Approximate time	3 hours	Ⓒ TL 785 346
Parking	Roadside parking at Castle Hedingham	Ⓓ TL 786 340
		Ⓔ TL 792 331
Ordnance Survey maps	Landranger 155 (Bury St Edmunds), Explorer 195 (Braintree & Saffron Walden)	Ⓕ TL 789 333
		Ⓖ TL 784 338

This figure-of-eight walk in the Colne Valley starts with a circuit of Castle Park, the wooded parkland surrounding the remains of Hedingham Castle. The rest of the route is across fields and through woodland, including a short but attractive stretch beside the placid River Colne. There are fine views over the valley but some parts of the walk are likely to be muddy and/or overgrown at times.

There are some delightful old houses and cottages in Castle Hedingham, which lies at the foot of the wooded hill occupied by the great castle. The church is an unusually fine and interesting example of an almost complete Norman village church, with a superb late 12th-century nave and chancel. At the east end is a rare Norman wheel window.

Hedingham Castle is one of the grandest and best preserved Norman keeps in the country. It was built in 1140 for the powerful De Veres, earls of Oxford, and still stands to its full height of 110 feet. Its interior probably gives visitors a better idea of a Norman castle than anywhere else, and the carved stonework and great cross arches in the great hall are normally only seen in the finest cathedrals.

📝 The walk begins in the main street by the **Bell Inn** and post office.

With your back to the inn, turn left, follow the road around a left-hand bend and turn right down Church Lane. Bend right, passing the church, and keep ahead along Crown Street to a T-junction Ⓐ. Take the path ahead – not the parallel drive to the right of it – which passes to the right of Pye Cottage, and this attractive, hedge- and tree-lined path heads gently uphill to a stile. After climbing it, keep ahead across a field to the end of a hedge, continue uphill alongside the hedge and pass through a kissing-gate at the top.

Turn right along a winding lane. After 600 yards at a public footpath sign opposite Rosemary Farm, turn right on to a path across a field. Carry on along a narrow enclosed path that heads downhill through woodland bordering Castle Park and pass beside a barrier on to a road. Turn left and look

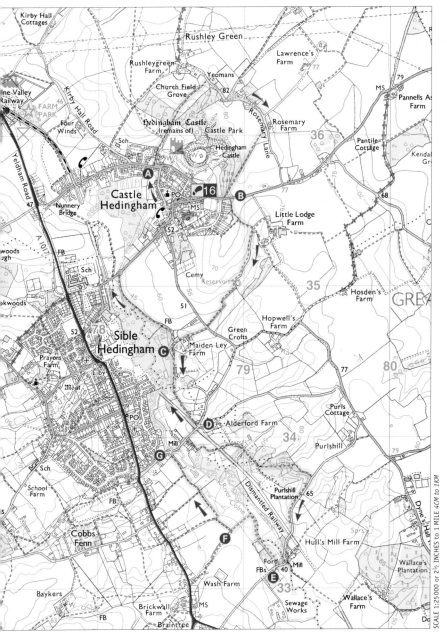

out for steps and a public footpath sign on the right **B**. Climb the steps and walk first along an enclosed path and then along a right-hand field edge to a waymarked post. Turn left, continue across the field towards a farm and head down into a dip, passing to the right of a solitary tree. Do not climb the

stile at the bottom of the field but turn right along its left-hand field edge and follow it – there are several twists and turns – to a road.

Cross over, walk along a tarmac track

The River Colne near Castle Hedingham

again. Turn right by Hull's Mill, a 19th-century rebuilding of an earlier mill, and just after crossing a footbridge over the River Colne by a ford, turn right through a kissing-gate **E**. Walk across a field to a hedge corner, keep by the hedge on the left to join the river, climb a stile and continue beside it past a field corner and at the end of the next field, at a waymarked post, turn left away from the river. Walk along the right-hand edge of fields and, on joining a track, turn right through a hedge gap **F** – here leaving the Hedingham Mills Walk – and follow a track at the edge of a field.

Continue along a path by the right-hand edge of the next two fields and, in the corner of the second field, pass through a belt of trees and keep ahead along an enclosed path. The path bears right through another belt of trees, crosses a footbridge and curves left to reach a lane in front of Alderford Mill **G**. The way continues to the right to cross a bridge over the Colne to meet your outward route. Retrace your steps to point **C** just before Maiden Ley Farm. Turn left here off the tarmac track and walk along a path that keeps along the right-hand edge of a pool. The path then winds through trees and bushes, crosses a plank footbridge and keeps along the right-hand edge of woodland. As you later continue along the left-hand edge of a field, the top of the keep of Hedingham Castle can be seen across the field to the right.

The path eventually reaches a road just to the right of a brick bridge. Turn right and follow it back into Castle Hedingham.

and, soon after passing to the right of Maiden Ley Farm, you join the well-waymarked Hedingham Mills Walk **C**. The track bears left and, where it ends, keep ahead along a grassy track and take the right-hand enclosed path along the left-hand edge of woodland, which turns right to a plank footbridge. Cross it and turn left to continue across rough meadowland, bear right to pass a house and keep ahead to a lane **D**. Turn right, cross a bridge over a disused railway track and, at a public footpath sign, turn left along a track, passing between cottages.

At a waymarked post, turn left to walk along the right-hand edge of a field, follow the edge as it curves first right and then left, pass beside a barrier and continue along a fence-lined path. Keep along the narrow, enclosed path to enter woodland and continue through it to a T-junction. Turn right along a track, at a fork keep ahead along the right-hand track and, follow the path as it heads gently uphill, re-enters trees and continues up through this most attractive woodland. It then turns right to keep along the left-hand edge of the wood and emerges, via a barrier, on to a lane.

Turn right down this narrow lane and cross a bridge over the disused railway

Benfleet Downs and Hadleigh Marsh

		GPS waypoints
Start	Salvation Army Hadleigh Farm	🖉 TQ 808 864
Distance	7½ miles (11.9km). Shorter version 5¾ miles (8.9km)	Ⓐ TQ 808 858
Height gain	655 feet (200m). Shorter version 510 feet (155m)	Ⓑ TQ 804 858
		Ⓒ TQ 801 868
Approximate time	3½ hours. Shorter version 2¾ hours	Ⓓ TQ 795 858
		Ⓔ TQ 779 858
		Ⓕ TQ 780 857
Parking	Hadleigh Farm Rare Breeds Centre car park (Pay and Display)	Ⓖ TQ 803 853
		Ⓗ TQ 817 858
Ordnance Survey maps	Landranger 178 (Thames Estuary), Explorer 175 (Southend-on-Sea & Basildon)	

From both the hilltop vantage points on this walk – Hadleigh Country Park and Hadleigh Castle – there are splendid views across Canvey Island and the Thames Estuary to the North Downs on the horizon, and along the river from Southend to Canary Wharf. The walk begins from the Salvation Army's Hadleigh Rare Breeds Farm, where you can see some of Britain's rare native breeds of goats and sheep. The nearby country park has a reconstructed Iron Age round house as well as hire facilities for its Olympic mountain bike trail, and the ruins of the 13th century Hadleigh Castle are also worthy of exploration.

🖉 Out of the car park, turn right along a narrow lane. Through a barrier at the end bear left on a track to Hadleigh Castle. The castle is visited at the end of the walk, so, for the time being, continue through a gate ahead, following the ongoing track downhill. Through another gate at the bottom Ⓐ, go right on a broad path at the edge of the marsh towards Benfleet.

After ¼ mile (400m), watch for a waypost indicating a path leaving through the right-hand hedge Ⓑ, which rises gently between fences. At the top are two adjacent kissing-gates. Go through the left-most one and continue

upwards, shortly reaching a crossing path, part of a mountain bike complex built for the 2012 Summer Olympics – so keep an eye open for bikes!

Walk ahead past an information board along a grass swathe to the end of a gravel track, which leads on up the hill. At a junction at the top, go briefly right past an exercise station and then turn left by a wooden post. Walk to a kissing-gate in front of abandoned buildings and continue along a grass track that runs below the high embankment of a reservoir. Emerge at the end onto a gravel track, which to the left, leads out to a tarmac

Hadleigh Castle

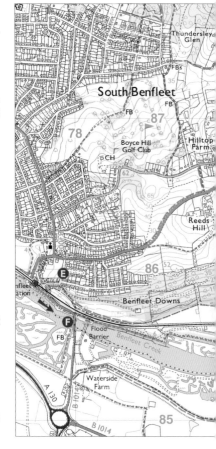

service road **C**.

Turn right to a junction and go left, passing the Hadleigh Country Park car park. Beyond a barrier, over to the right, is a reconstruction of an Iron Age round house. The route, however, continues ahead beyond the end of the drive to a kissing-gate into the country park.

To the left, a track drops through trees, shortly passing through a gate into the corner of rough meadowland. A swathe leads on down the hill, closing with the trees to the right to reach the bottom corner. Ignoring a kissing-gate, keep ahead through a gap and continue at the edge of two more fields to leave through a gate onto a crossing track. Cross to another gate opposite and keep ahead at the edge of scrub grazing to emerge at the far end onto a gravel path **D**.

To the right, the path winds on at the edge of the grazing marsh, later rising onto higher ground across the slopes of Benfleet Downs. Keep going as it is then joined by other tracks and finally turns out onto the corner of a street in Benfleet **E**. Go left to the bottom and then right in front of the railway station. After a few yards, swing left through an underpass beneath the track and go left again along the main road. As that then bends to cross the river, keep ahead on a lane **F**, signed as a path to Leigh.

Walk on past a flood barrier and Benfleet Moorings. Bending left, the drive finally ends at a gate. Carry on along a track signed to Hadleigh Castle. After 1 mile (1.6km), it sweeps around a left bend. At the subsequent right bend **G**, drop left off the track to a stile and follow a trod across rough grazing to a railway crossing.

Cross with care and bear right over more pasture to join a gravel path.

Follow it right, shortly passing junction **B**. Keep going to **A**, where you can shorten the walk by reversing your outward steps up past Hadleigh Castle. However, for the full walk and some more fine views, carry on along the track for a further half mile at the edge of the marsh. Eventually, pass through a gate to a fork **H**. Branch left to a signpost and go left again through consecutive gates bounding a ditch. The path ahead rises steadily along the shoulder of the hill. Towards the top, the castle comes into view. Pass through a kissing-gate to find an entrance to the castle through a gate on the left. Walk on past the ruins to leave the grounds at the far right corner. Turn right and walk back along your outward route to the car park. ●

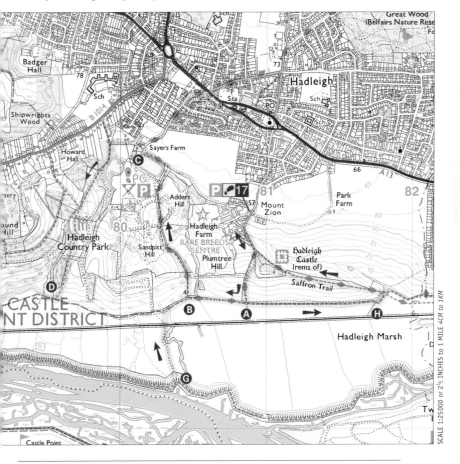

Mill Green and Blackmore

		GPS waypoints
Start	Millgreen Common, parking area on the common almost opposite the Cricketers pub	🖉 TL 639 012
		Ⓐ TL 638 014
Distance	6¾ miles (11km)	Ⓑ TL 635 028
Height gain	225 feet (70m)	Ⓒ TL 622 029
Approximate time	3¼ hours	Ⓓ TL 611 027
Parking	Millgreen Common	Ⓔ TL 605 027
		Ⓕ TL 605 018
Ordnance Survey maps	Landranger 167 (Chelmsford), Explorer 183 (Chelmsford & The Rodings)	Ⓖ TL 625 014
		Ⓗ TL 630 018

Much of the walk is through attractive woodlands which, like Millgreen Common, are surviving remnants of Writtle Forest. In between there are extensive views over open country, and the route passes through the attractive village of Blackmore with its fine medieval church. Most of the route is along broad and clear tracks but there are some narrow paths in places.

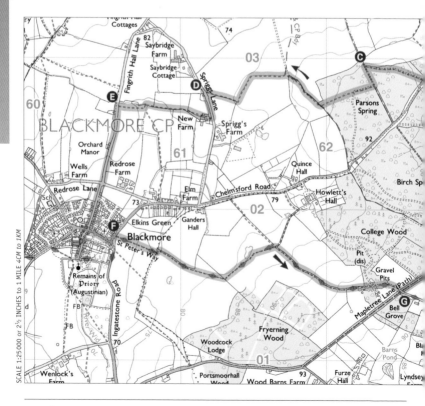

Millgreen Common is a small remnant of the medieval royal hunting ground of Writtle Forest, and its landscape of woodland and open grassland can have changed little since the Middle Ages.

🖊 Start by returning to the road almost opposite **The Cricketers** pub, turn left along the road for about ¼ mile and, at a bridleway sign after a cottage, turn left **A**.

Follow this undulating track to where it emerges from the trees and keep ahead across a field to a road. Turn left, follow the road around a right-hand bend and, at a public bridleway sign, turn left **B** along a broad track (Metsons Lane), passing beside a timber yard. Continue along the right-hand, inside edge of Barrow Wood to a road, cross over to a public footpath sign and walk along a path through more woodland to reach a concrete track **C**. Turn left and, after about 100 yards, turn right over a plank footbridge and continue along a winding path through dense woodland. Turn left to cross a plank footbridge and climb a stile to emerge from the trees.

Turn right, climb another stile and continue along the right-hand edge of rough grassland and, at the far, tapering corner of the field, keep ahead to cross a stile and continue along the right-hand edge of the next field. Follow the field edge to the left, turn right over a footbridge, turn along the left-hand edge of the next field and, in the corner, turn right and continue along the left-hand field edge to a lane **D**. Turn left along the tree-lined lane and, at a public footpath sign, turn right on to a track, passing between farm buildings to a gate. Go through, keep ahead and cross a stile at another gate and continue along the left-hand edge of a field.

Go over a stile, cross a plank footbridge, keep along the left-hand edge of the next field but, after about 20 yards, turn left through another hedge gap and climb a stile. Continue by the right-hand field edge, at a fence corner keep ahead across the field to regain the field edge and go through a kissing-gate and over a plank footbridge on to a lane **E**. Turn left and at a crossroads keep ahead into Blackmore to reach another crossroads in the village centre.

The route continues to the left but it is worthwhile first keeping ahead along picturesque Church Street to visit Blackmore's mainly Norman church. Its most striking feature is the tall, pagoda-shaped, 15th-century timber tower and spire. The church was originally built to serve an Augustinian priory and became a parish church after the priory, of which there are virtually no remains, was dissolved in 1527. Henry VIII was a

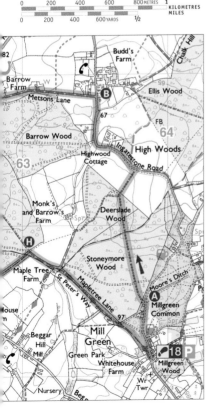

| 0 | 200 | 400 | 600 | 800 METRES | 1 |
| 0 | 200 | 400 | 600 YARDS | ½ | KILOMETRES / MILES |

frequent visitor to Blackmore as he had a mistress here.

Go back to the crossroads and turn right along The Green to a T-junction, turn left and, at a public footpath sign, turn right **F** through a hedge gap and walk across a field, making for a waymarked post on the far side. Go through a hedge gap, turn left along the left-hand edge of the next field, follow the edge to the right and, at a hedge corner, keep ahead across the field to a footpath post. Go through another hedge gap, bear slightly left across the next field, skirting the right-hand edge of a pond, and continue across to a

In Blackmore

track on the far side. Turn right to continue first along the left-hand edge of fields, and then through woodland, (passing to the left of a pond belonging to Stoney Lodge) and bear right to reach a stile by a crossroads **G**.

Go over the stile and turn left on to a bridlepath that keeps along the right-hand, inside edge of College Wood to a T-junction and turn right **H** in the Mapletree Lane direction, along a broad, tree-lined track. At a fork, take the right-hand track, which continues along the right-hand, inside edge of more fine woodland and, where it bears left, keep ahead beside a barrier and take the grassy path across Millgreen Common to return to the start. ●

Coggeshall and Feering

		GPS waypoints	
Start	Coggeshall		TL 850 226
Distance	7½ miles (12.25km)	Ⓐ	TL 856 229
Height gain	320 feet (100m)	Ⓑ	TL 870 233
Approximate time	3½ hours	Ⓒ	TL 869 229
Parking	Coggeshall	Ⓓ	TL 869 219
Ordnance Survey maps	Landranger 168 (Colchester), Explorer 195 (Braintree & Saffron Walden)	Ⓔ	TL 876 212
		Ⓕ	TL 872 205
		Ⓖ	TL 867 212
		Ⓗ	TL 855 208
		Ⓙ	TL 851 215

This is a walk of wide and extensive views in the gentle landscape of the Blackwater Valley to the east and south of Coggeshall. It is mostly across fields and there is a particularly attractive stretch beside the river near the end. Historic interest is provided by the fine medieval churches at Coggeshall and Feering, plus Paycocke's House and the monastic barn and chapel near Coggeshall.

In the Middle Ages, Coggeshall was second only to Colchester in Essex as a prosperous centre of the cloth trade and it has a number of attractive, timber-framed buildings that reflect this. Largest and most impressive of these is Paycocke's, built around 1500 by Thomas Paycocke, a wealthy merchant clothier. The clock tower in the town centre was built to commemorate Queen Victoria's Golden Jubilee in 1887.

🖉 Start at the junction of roads in the town centre and walk along Church Street, passing to the right of the large 15th-century 'wool church'. Reaching a mini-roundabout, turn right. Passing St Anne's Close, turn off left Ⓐ through a gate to join the Essex Way. Walk along a narrow, tree-lined path and keep ahead across a field. Pass through a hedge gap and continue along the left-hand edge of the next field. Go through another hedge gap and ascend steps to the main road. Cross over, descend steps opposite, climb a stile

and walk along a left-hand field edge.

Keep ahead at a junction to continue along the left-hand edge of the next field but after about ½ mile look out for where an Essex Way sign directs you to turn left down steps. Go through a hedge gap, cross a plank footbridge and turn right along a right-hand field edge. On reaching a lane, turn right Ⓑ – here leaving the Essex Way – to a junction with a main road. Go right and then cross to take the first left, Old Road Ⓒ. Where the lane curves slightly left, bear right to a public bridleway sign and walk along a tree shaded enclosed path. A stretch along the right-hand edge of a field is followed by another enclosed path before emerging on to a lane Ⓓ. Turn left to a T-junction and turn right, in the Feering and Kelvedon direction, along a narrow, winding lane.

After about ¾ mile (1.2km) – just after passing South Cottage – turn off right Ⓔ at a public footpath sign. Follow a grassy path that heads across

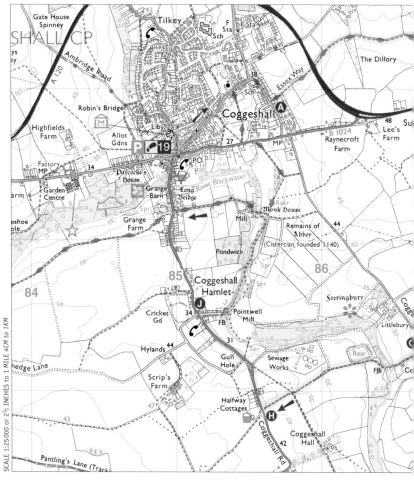

fields, later continuing by a right-hand field edge. After going through a hedge

gap, bear left and walk diagonally across a field towards Feering church,

The River Blackwater

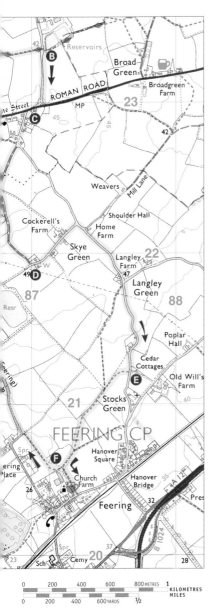

beside the left edge of the next field and keep ahead, passing through a hedge gap, to a road. Turn right and, after about ½ mile (800m), at a public footpath sign, turn left along a track **G**. Where the track ends at a cottage, continue through trees along the right-hand one of two paths ahead and cross a footbridge over the River Blackwater. Keep ahead to enter a field but, after a few yards along its right-hand edge, turn right over a plank footbridge and turn left along an enclosed path. The route now continues along the left-hand edge of a succession of fields – there is a track at one point – finally going through a gate on to a road opposite the **The Halfway** restaurant **H**.

Turn right into Coggeshall Hamlet and at a No Through Road sign, turn right **J** along Pointwell Lane. Where the lane ends, keep ahead along a track, passing in front of the former Pointwell Mill, and cross a bridge over the river. Bear right to cross another bridge and go through a gate. Now follows a delightful part of the route as you walk across meadows beside the tree-lined bank of the Blackwater. Cross a foot-bridge over the channel that has been on your right, keep ahead and, at the end of the meadow, climb a stile and continue to a T-junction.

Turn left along a track, recross the river, bear right through a farmyard and continue along the track, passing to the left of an isolated 13th-century chapel. This was the gatehouse chapel of the now vanished Coggeshall Abbey. The track reaches a road in front of Cogge-shall Grange Barn, another monastic survival. Now owned by the National Trust, it dates from the 12th century and is reputedly the oldest surviving timber-framed barn in Europe.

At the road turn right, cross the Blackwater once more and keep ahead into Coggeshall. ●

pass through a wide gap and continue across to the corner of the next field **F**. For a short detour into Feering, turn left along the right-hand field edge and turn right along a road into the pleasant village, which has a pub, **The Bell Inn**, and 15th- to 16th-century church.

Retrace your steps to point **F** and continue along the left-hand edge of the next field. At a waymarked post turn right across a field. Then walk

Newport and Debden

Newport and Debden

		GPS waypoints	
Start	Newport, station car park	🖾	TL 522 335
Distance	6½ miles (10.5km)	Ⓐ	TL 537 329
Height gain	475 feet (145m)	Ⓑ	TL 552 323
Approximate time	3¼ hours	Ⓒ	TL 553 332
Parking	Newport station, Pay and Display	Ⓓ	TL 545 338
Ordnance Survey maps	Landrangers 154 (Cambridge & Newmarket) and 167 (Chelmsford), Explorer 195 (Braintree & Saffron Walden)	Ⓔ	TL 521 342

By Essex standards this is a relatively hilly walk, rising to 345 feet on the first part of the route between Newport and Debden. The return leg takes you across part of Debden Park and then on through the valley of Debden Water. Both Newport and Debden are attractive places with fine medieval churches.

The long main street in Newport is lined by handsome buildings dating from the late medieval period to the 19th century. Foremost among these is the brick and timber-framed, 15th-century Monk's Barn. The 13th- to 15th-century church has an imposing tower built in 1858.

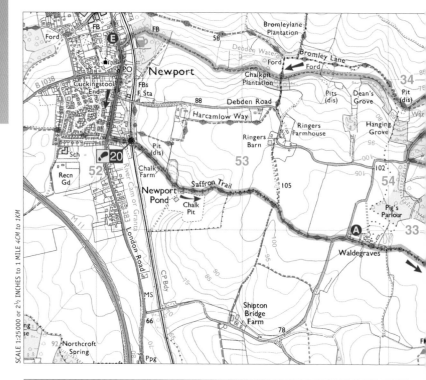

✏ Start by crossing the station footbridge, keep ahead to a tarmac track and turn right. At a public bridleway sign by the entrance to a huge chalk quarry, turn left along a pleasant, hedge - and tree-lined path, which heads uphill to emerge into a field. Keep along the left-hand edge of the field, following it as it curves right, and eventually reaches a lane. Turn left and, where the lane turns left, keep ahead Ⓐ along the track to Waldegraves Farm.

Continue along the track, passing along the right-hand edge of Cabbage Wood. At a fork take the right-hand track to continue by the edge of the wood. Look out for where a waymarked post directs you to turn first left and then right and then head gently downhill along the right-hand edge of a field to reach a lane by a picturesque, black and white thatched cottage.

Turn left. After 300 yards, and at a permissive footpath sign, turn left again Ⓑ to walk along the right-hand edge of a field. Just before reaching the corner, turn right over a footbridge and turn left to keep along the left-hand edge of the next field, by woodland on the left. The path continues first along the right-hand, inside edge and later the left-hand, inside edge of the woodland, then becomes enclosed and bears left through a hedge gap. Turn right along the right-hand field edge, follow the edge to the left and continue up to a lane Ⓒ. Turn right here for a short detour into the pretty village of Debden which has a pond, thatched cottages and a pub, **The Plough**, at the eastern end of High Street.

Retrace your steps along the lane and continue to the entrance to Debden churchyard. The church, which stands in a beautiful and isolated setting, dates mainly from the 13th century. Bear right along a waymarked path by the right-hand edge of the churchyard, and follow the path, which passes a kissing-gate to the churchyard and later crosses a bridge over the neck of a lake. Keep ahead along a track and, at a footpath sign, turn right to follow a path across Debden Park. To the right is a view of the lake.

At the far end of the field, keep ahead and walk along the left-hand edge of the next field and keep ahead to go through another kissing-gate on to a road. Turn right downhill, cross Debden Water and continue gently uphill to a public footpath sign Ⓓ. Turn left here and, at a fork immediately ahead, take the left-hand track. Climb a stile, walk along a driveway, climb another stile and keep along the left-hand edge of the next field to go through a gate on the left. The path now curves along the right-hand field edge. Go over a stile. At a fork take the left-hand path, pass

through a gap into the next field and curve left by the edge of woodland to continue across the middle of the field to a stile.

Climb it, keep ahead across a field, making for the corner of trees, and continue by the trees to a crossing of paths. Keep ahead beside conifers to the corner of the field and continue gently uphill along a broad, grassy ride between trees. As you keep along the winding right-hand edge of the next field, by trees on the right, the top of the tower of Newport church comes into view. In the field corner, keep ahead through a plantation, turn left to cross a footbridge over the infant River Cam and turn right to continue under a railway bridge.

Keep ahead along a tarmac track to the main street in Newport and turn left **E**. At the far end of the village, turn left again to return to the station. ●

A lane near Debden

Stour Valley: Constable Country

		GPS waypoints	
Start	Manningtree station	🖉	TM 094 322
Distance	7¼ miles (11.75km)	Ⓐ	TM 092 321
Height gain	350 feet (105m)	Ⓑ	TM 080 315
Approximate time	3½ hours	Ⓒ	TM 066 318
Parking	Manningtree station	Ⓓ	TM 059 319
Ordnance Survey maps	Landranger 168 (Colchester),	Ⓔ	TM 057 331
	Explorer 196 (Sudbury, Hadleigh	Ⓕ	TM 057 336
	& Dedham Vale)	Ⓖ	TM 067 337
		Ⓗ	TM 075 333

This classic walk is in the Stour Valley on the Essex–Suffolk border, immortalised in the paintings of John Constable. An undulating route along the well-waymarked Essex Way, mainly via tracks and field paths, brings you to Dedham. The walk then continues by the winding River Stour through Dedham Vale, the heart of Constable Country, passing the landmarks of Flatford Mill and Willy Lott's Cottage before returning to the start. Pick a fine day and take time to enjoy this outstanding walk to the full.

🖉 With your back to the station building, head diagonally right to the lower car park and take the path, signposted to Flatford and Dedham, down to a T-junction and turn right along a tree-lined track. At a footpath post, turn left Ⓐ in the Lawford church direction, along an enclosed path, which heads steadily uphill, bends right and then left to reach the church.

Go through a gate into the churchyard, pass to the right of the church and the path bears left to exit the churchyard by another gate. Head across to public footpath and Essex Way signs, bear right to a field corner and continue into trees to a kissing-gate. Go through and head diagonally right to go through another one. Turn left along the straight, tarmac track, pass beside a gate and turn right along a road.

Follow the road around a left-hand bend and after ¼ mile, bear left Ⓑ at a public bridleway sign, along an enclosed track to a gate. Go through, and continue along the enclosed track. Follow it left through a gate and walk past a cottage. Follow the ongoing track, swinging around a right-hand bend and past a junction, keep ahead at a crossroads and the track bears right down to a farm. At an Essex Way sign, bear right off the track, walk across grass to enter woodland and continue gently downhill to cross a plank footbridge.

Climb a stile, keep ahead across a field to climb another, carefully cross a railway line, climb a stile and go through a kissing-gate and keep straight ahead across a field to another kissing-gate. Go through and keep ahead between fences to go through a further kissing-gate. Continue along an enclosed path to a road. Cross over, go through the kissing-gate opposite, bear slightly left across a field to the corner and climb a stile on to a lane.

Turn right and the lane curves left and continues through trees. Where it bends right, keep ahead **C** through a kissing-gate, head gently uphill along the left-hand edge of a field to go through a gate, and keep ahead over the brow to go through another kissing-gate later followed by a gate. Walk along an enclosed grassy path, go through a kissing-gate and continue across the middle of the next field, then along an enclosed path. In the corner, go through a gate and keep ahead along a track to a road. Turn right. After 100 yards, leave over a stile on the left **D** and walk

across a field, heading down into woodland. Climb a stile and keep along the bottom, inside edge of the wood, turning left to pass in front of a house.

Turn right along a drive to a tarmac track, and turn right, passing cottages. After 120 yards, at a public footpath sign, turn left along a tarmac track between more cottages. Go through a gate, pass in front of a farmhouse, and turn right through another gate. Keep ahead to a stile. After climbing it, walk along the left-hand edge of a field. Through a gate, cross a plank footbridge, bear right and head diagonally across the next field. Cross a plank footbridge and climb a stile in the corner. Head across two fields, going through a kissing-gate and continue along a right-hand field edge.

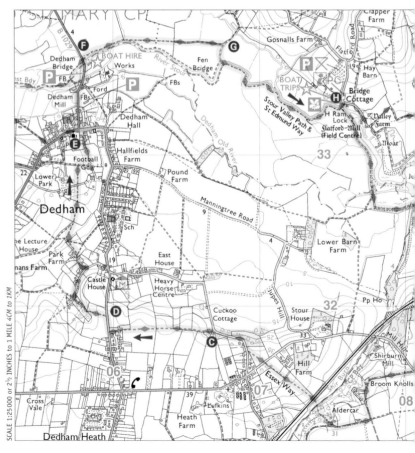

In the field corner, keep ahead to climb a stile into a sports field and turn right along its right-hand edge, passing behind the cricket pavilion, to a tarmac path. Turn left along the tree-lined path, passing beside a barrier to emerge on to a road in the centre of Dedham **E**.

From the 14th to the 17th centuries this small town was a flourishing centre of the cloth trade and has a wealth of attractive buildings. The large 'wool church' was built in 1492 and has an imposing west tower. Constable attended the local grammar school.

Keep ahead along Mill Lane, passing Dedham Mill and cross bridges over first a channel, then the main River Stour and finally another channel, here briefly entering Suffolk. At a public footpath sign to East Bergholt and Flatford, turn right **F** through a kissing-gate and walk across riverside meadows beside the Stour, later bearing away from the river to a kissing-gate on the far side of the meadow. Keep ahead along a tree-lined path to a T-junction, turn sharp right **G** on to another tree-lined path and go

through a kissing-gate to cross Fen Bridge over the Stour, here re-entering Essex.

Turn left down steps and go through another kissing-gate. Now comes a delightful part of the walk as you continue across meadows by the winding river through a typical Constable landscape. After going through a kissing-gate in front of a wooden footbridge **H** the route continues to the right, still beside the river, but it is worthwhile crossing the bridge to Bridge Cottage and turning right along a lane for a short distance to see Flatford Mill and Willy Lott's Cottage.

All these National Trust properties feature in Constable's paintings. Bridge Cottage houses a Constable exhibition and has a pleasant tearoom. Both Flatford Mill and Willy Lott's Cottage are leased to the Field Studies Council and are not open to the public. Constable's father owned Flatford Mill and others in the Stour Valley.

After turning right in front of the footbridge, at a public footpath sign to Manningtree, walk along a tree-lined path, passing Flatford Lock. A little farther on is a fine view across the river of Flatford Mill. Continue along the path and later you pass to the right of a concrete barrier. Cross a bridge over a channel by a lock, go through a kissing-gate and keep ahead beside the barrier to another kissing-gate. Turn left through it and walk along the top of a low embankment above pastures and marshland. Go through two more kissing-gates and, just after the second one, turn right at a public footpath sign to Manningtree station.

Go through another kissing-gate and along an enclosed path that turns first left and then right, widens into a track and passes under a railway bridge. Just beyond the bridge, turn left along a tree-lined track parallel to the embankment, which leads back to the start. ●

0	200	400	600	800 METRES	1
				KILOMETRES MILES	
0	200	400	600 YARDS	½	

Audley Park and Wendens Ambo

		GPS waypoints	
Start	Saffron Walden		TL 538 385
Distance	7½ miles (12.1km)	**A**	TL 534 382
Height gain	490 feet (150m)	**B**	TL 520 385
Approximate time	3½ hours	**C**	TL 524 380
Parking	Long stay car park in Saffron Walden for the full walk	**D**	TL 518 369
		E	TL 511 362
		F	TL 519 361
Ordnance Survey maps	Landranger 154 (Cambridge & Newmarket), Explorer 195 (Braintree & Saffron Walden)	**G**	TL 530 379

Saffron Walden is situated at the gates of Audley Park, and you quickly gain access to paths that take you across the splendid parkland and over the River Cam, with grand views of Audley End House. The route then heads across to the picturesque village of Wendens Ambo, on the other side of the valley, before returning for a final stroll across the park. A circuit of Audley Park gives the option of a short walk omitting Wendens Ambo. Leave plenty of time to explore Saffron Walden, a most appealing town.

Saffron Walden is an outstandingly attractive town with a wealth of fine old buildings, a reflection of its importance and prosperity in the Middle Ages as a centre of the cloth industry. It was also the main centre for the production of the saffron crocus – hence the word saffron in the name of the town – grown locally as a medicine and as a dye for the cloth trade. Dominating the town is the magnificent church, a tall and spacious building of cathedral-like proportions, mostly built between 1450 and 1525. The spire was added in 1832. Nearby are the remains of the Norman castle keep and a medieval turf maze. Be sure to take a look at the fascinating **Old Sun Inn**, a group of 14th-century houses with some outstanding pargetting (moulded plasterwork) from

the 17th century.

Start in the Market Place by the late 18th-century Town Hall (now the tourist information centre) and, facing the library, walk along the street to the left of it. Turn left at a T-junction, take the first turning on the right (Abbey Lane), and pass some almshouses and keep ahead to go through a metal gate, here entering the Audley End estate **A**.

At a fork immediately ahead, take the right-hand path and at the next fork take the right-hand (narrower) path again and follow it across Audley Park. Cross a footbridge, pass through a line of trees and continue between fences to a kissing-gate. Go through, and the path continues along the right-hand edge of the park, gradually curving left. Over to the left are fine views of Audley End

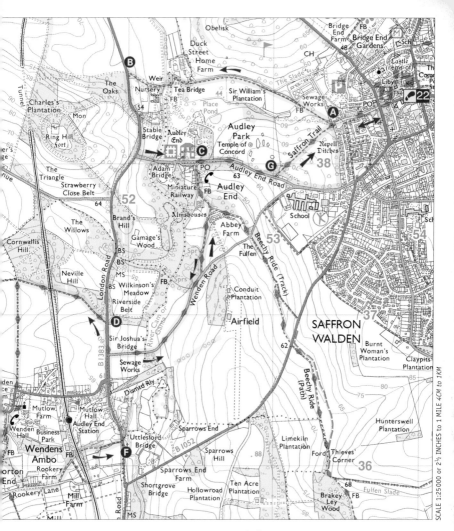

```
0        200     400     600     800 METRES  1
                                             KILOMETRES
                                             MILES
0        200     400     600 YARDS           ½
```

House. After just under ¹/₂ mile bear right to go through a metal kissing-gate beside a concrete bridge and walk along a tree-shaded path between a wall on the left, and a stream, to join a tarmac drive.

Keep along the drive, cross a bridge over the River Cam and continue up to a road **B**. Turn left along the roadside path and take the first lane on the left, cross Adam Bridge – from here there is a superb view of the house – and continue past the visitor entrance to Audley End House to a tarmac track on the right, signposted to the College of

St Mark **C**.

Audley End House, an outstanding example of Jacobean architecture, was built in the early 17th century by Lord Howard of Walden, 1st Earl of Suffolk, on the site of a medieval abbey. It was a huge palace, one of the largest in the country – almost twice its present size – and was even a royal palace for a while, bought by Charles II in 1669 but returned to the Howard family in 1701. In the 18th century it was partially demolished and then remodelled, with some of the rooms designed by Robert Adam. The formal gardens are superb, and the park, one of the finest in the country, was landscaped by Capability Brown.

Wendens Ambo

Continue along the lane if doing the short walk.

For the full walk, turn right gently downhill along the tarmac track, passing between rows of attractive old cottages, and at a fork in front of the college entrance, take the left-hand track. Where the track turns left, keep ahead across grass, by a wall on the right, to a waymarked post and follow more of these posts through a yard. Continue along the right-hand edge of a field, by woodland on the right, to a road and turn right. The road bears right to cross the River Cam again and heads up to a T-junction. Turn right and, at a public footpath sign at the corner of a wood, turn left **D** through a gate and walk along the right-hand edge of a field, by the woodland on the right.

In the field corner, keep ahead to cross a railway bridge, continue along the right-hand edge of the next field but, just before the field edge bears slightly left, turn left and head straight across the field. From this reasonably elevated position there are fine all-round views. Continue down a sunken, hedge-lined track to a road in the village of Wendens Ambo and keep ahead. On the left you pass a lane, lined on one side by picturesque thatched cottages, that leads to the attractive flint church. This dates from the 12th century and retains its Norman tower but was partially rebuilt and extended later in the Middle Ages.

Where the road curves right to the **Bell Inn**, turn left along a lane and, just after crossing a footbridge by a ford, turn left over a stile **E**. Walk along the right-hand field edge, negotiate two stiles in quick succession (plus the intervening plank footbridge) and bear left across a field to go through a gate. Keep in the same direction across the next field and on the far side cross a track to a waymarked gate. Go through, climb a stile a few yards ahead, continue along a fence-lined path, go through a gate and turn left to a lane.

Turn left along this narrow lane and, at a public footpath sign, bear left along a fence-lined path. Keep ahead through trees, turn right at a fork to pass under a railway viaduct and continue, by a stream on the left, to a stile. Climb it, keep beside the stream to climb another stile, continue along a fence-lined path and climb a stile on to a road **F**. Turn left. Shortly after passing the **Fighting Cocks** pub, turn right along the road signposted to Saffron Walden and Audley End House.

At this point you rejoin the outward route and retrace your steps to the lane in front of Audley End House **C**.

Turn right – here leaving the outward route and rejoining the short walk – keep by the boundary wall of Audley Park on the left and, after just over $^1/_4$ mile, turn left through a metal gate and under an arch to re-enter the estate **G**. Walk across the park in a straight line towards the buildings of Saffron Walden – the church spire can be seen ahead – and after going through a metal gate on the far side, retrace your steps through the town to the start. ●

Ingatestone and Mountnessing

		GPS waypoints	
Start	Ingatestone	🖉	TQ 651 996
Distance	8¼ miles (13.25km)	**A**	TQ 652 987
Height gain	390 feet (120m)	**B**	TQ 640 987
Approximate time	4 hours	**C**	TQ 636 988
Parking	Ingatestone	**D**	TQ 631 978
Ordnance Survey maps	Landranger 167 (Chelmsford),	**E**	TQ 634 974
	Explorer 175 (Southend-on-Sea	**F**	TQ 649 966
	& Basildon)	**G**	TQ 650 975
		H	TQ 651 981
		J	TQ 664 986

There are wide and unimpeded views on this highly enjoyable walk in the undulating country that lies just to the north of Brentwood and Billericay, and there is a real feel of solitude at times. It is also full of interest and includes two halls, three churches and a windmill. The route is on good paths and is well-waymarked throughout.

Ingatestone's long high street is lined by a mixture of buildings, including timber-framed ones dating from the 16th and 17th centuries and some fine Georgian houses. The small, pleasant town is dominated by the tall, red brick tower of its imposing medieval church, and inside are tombs of the Petre family, who lived in the nearby hall.

🖉 The walk starts in the main street in front of the church. Take the path up to it, bear right in front of it and go through a kissing-gate into a recreation ground. Keep ahead along a tarmac path but at a fence corner on the left, bear left to continue along the edge of a cricket field and turn right at another hedge corner to cross a railway bridge. Pass beside a metal fence, bear right and keep ahead across fields to a footpath post. Keep by the left-hand field edge, along an avenue of horse chestnut trees and at a fork by a fence corner **A** continue along the right-hand path,

bearing right to emerge on to a lane in front of Ingatestone Hall. The house, built in the 16th century by Sir William Petre, has an impressive long gallery and some fine Tudor panelling.

Turn left, at a public footpath sign turn right and walk along the right-hand field edge and go through a hedge gap. Keep ahead across the next field. At the far side, wind to an underpass beneath the railway. Beyond, walk between houses to emerge onto a street. Turn left for 150 yards, to find an enclosed tarmac track, marked Brentwood Circular Walk, signed off to the right. Continue along a road past a crossroads to a T-junction.

Turn right, and then immediately turn left **B** along the B1002. Shortly beyond a bridge over the A12, turn right along Trueloves Lane. Follow the lane around a left-hand bend and, at a public footpath sign, turn left **C** on to a path that heads gently downhill across

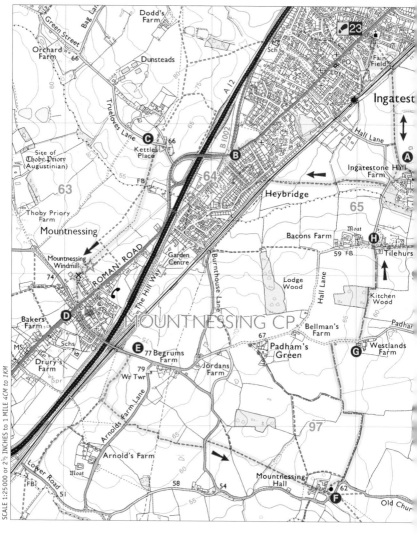

a field. The houses and windmill at Mountnessing can be seen on the ridge ahead. After crossing a footbridge over a brook, continue gently uphill, and the path bears right to head towards the windmill. At the far end of the field, go through a hedge gap into Coronation Playing Field and turn left to pass to the left of the early 19th-century windmill. Pass between gateposts, keep ahead to go through a fence gap and at the corner of a hedge, bear left across the playing field to emerge at a road junction in Mountnessing **D**.

Cross to continue along Church Road (signposted to Billericay). Shortly after re-crossing both the A12 and the railway line, turn right **E** at a public footpath sign and walk across a field, passing to the right of two isolated trees. Keep ahead beside a ditch to a waymarked post, turn left to cross a footbridge over the ditch and continue across a field to a lane. Cross over and take the path almost opposite across the next field passing to the left of a waymarked telegraph pole, to emerge on to another lane. Turn left and, at a public footpath sign, turn right and head straight across fields towards Mountnessing church, crossing two footbridges. Continue along a track,

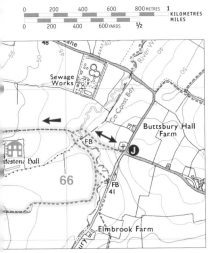

passing farm buildings and in front of Mountnessing Hall, continue along a tarmac drive, and turn left through a gate to enter the churchyard. At the far corner of the churchyard, go through a hedge gap to reach a track **F**. The 13th-century church served the medieval manor of Mountnessing, based on the hall, which is why it is some distance from the present village. The hall was the home of the Mountneys, who gave their name to the area, and the present building is mainly Elizabethan with a Georgian façade.

Turn left and walk along the right-hand edge of a field. Turn left in the field corner, at a T-junction turn right and continue along a tree-lined path. Keep ahead along a track across fields to the right of a ditch and, where the track bends right in front of a house, continue along an enclosed path to a lane. Turn right. After 200 yards, at a public bridleway sign, turn left **G** on a track between fields. At a waymarked

post, bear right to continue along the left-hand edge of the next field, by Kitchen Wood on the left. Turn right in the corner and, where the hedge on the left ends, turn left to keep along the right-hand edge of a field. Turn right **H** on to a concrete track – soon Ingatestone Hall is seen over to the left – and where this track ends, turn left along a path by a ditch on the right.

Follow the ditch to the right, turn left in the field corner and continue alongside the meandering River Wid. Ignore a footbridge and carry on, later crossing a side ditch. To visit Buttsbury church, the wooden tower of which has been in sight for much of the last ¹/₂ mile (800m), turn right over the adjacent footbridge spanning the river, turn right and at the corner head up across the field to the church **J**. This small, isolated church has a 14th century nave and an 18th-century chancel.

Otherwise, turn left from the river along a track across fields to Ingatestone Hall, where Elizabeth I stayed in the 16th century. Just before reaching some barns, bear right along the right-hand field edge and bear right again on joining another path **A**. Here you rejoin the outward route and retrace your steps to the start.

Mountnessing windmill

Burnham and the River Crouch

Start	Burnham-on-Crouch	**GPS waypoints**	
Distance	8½ miles (13.6km)	✎ TQ 952 955	
Height gain	225 feet (70m)	Ⓐ TQ 979 953	
Approximate time	4 hours	Ⓑ TQ 961 969	
Parking	Burnham-on-Crouch	Ⓒ TQ 947 973	
Ordnance Survey maps	Landranger 168 (Colchester), Explorer 176 (Blackwater Estuary)	Ⓓ TQ 938 974	
		Ⓔ TQ 935 969	
		Ⓕ TQ 937 955	

The first and last parts of the walk are along promenades and embankments beside the River Crouch and there are wide views, looking across the estuary to the desolate and uninhabited marshes of Wallasea Island on the other side. In between, the route heads inland across fields and along lanes, doing a loop around the edge of Burnham and passing its imposing medieval church, about one mile north of the present town centre.

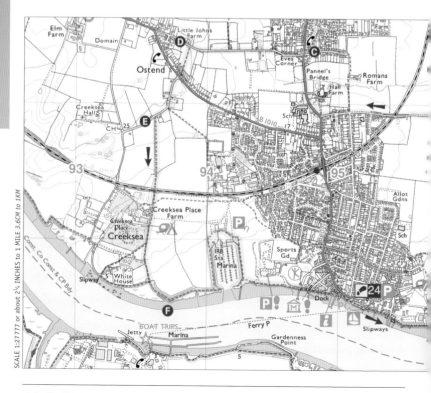

SCALE 1:27 777 or about 2¼ INCHES to 1 MILE 3.6CM to 1KM

Many handsome and attractive old buildings line the river and quayside at Burnham-on-Crouch. The town developed as a port in the Middle Ages when the original settlement moved away from the church to the river.

The walk begins in the town centre by the Victorian Clock Tower. Turn down Shore Road (signposted to Ferry and Quay) to the river and turn left along the paved promenade beside it. After the promenade ends, keep ahead along the top of the sea wall, following it around several small creeks. There are fine and expansive views both inland over reclaimed marshland and across the estuary. After about 2 miles (3.2km), look out for a stile below on the left and descend from the embankment – there are some steps cut into the turf – to climb it **A**.

Walk along a track, by a drainage channel on the left, and where the track turns right, keep ahead along a path, still beside the channel. In the field corner bear left to join another track and, after passing a public footpath sign, the route continues along a straight concrete track across fields. Ignore the first public footpath sign on the right but, at the second one, turn right along the left-hand edge of a field. Turn left at a way-marked post, continue along a straight path, passing an isolated tree, and at a T-junction, turn right along the left-hand edge of a field, beside a line of trees.

Pass through a hedge gap, keep straight ahead across the next field and, on the far side, turn right along a track. Turn left towards a farm, passing through the yard to emerge onto a narrow lane **B**. Turn left, cross a railway bridge and keep ahead to a T-junction. Turn right, passing Burnham's large and impressive mainly 14th-century church, and at a crossroads turn left along Green Lane **C**. After just over ¹/₂ mile (800m), turn

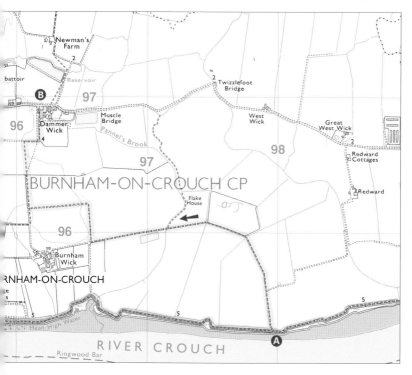

left  **D** over a plank footbridge, at a public footpath sign Creeksea No.2, and walk along a path to a road. Cross to Creeksea Lane opposite, following it around a right curve. Just beyond a large house, turn off left at a footpath sign **E** and walk along the right-hand edge of a field. Keep ahead across the next field to cross a railway line and continue along the right-hand edge of fields towards the River Crouch. On reaching the riverside embankment, bear left along it **F** and, apart from having to make a wide detour around a marina, you keep by the river back to Burnham.

After the marina, the route continues along a tarmac path and, on reaching the town, the path twists and turns between boatyards, cottages and along the quayside. Between **Ye Olde White Harte** Hotel and the **Anchor**, turn left along Shore Road to return to the starting point.

Burnham-on-Crouch

Maldon and the Blackwater Estuary

Start	Maldon, Promenade Park	
Distance	8¾ miles (14km)	
Height gain	355 feet (110m)	
Approximate time	4½ hours	
Parking	Promenade Park at Maldon	
Ordnance Survey maps	Landranger 168 (Colchester), Explorer 183 (Chelmsford & The Rodings)	

GPS waypoints

- TL 862 064
- Ⓐ TL 857 067
- Ⓑ TL 849 070
- Ⓒ TL 838 077
- Ⓓ TL 845 079
- Ⓔ TL 872 068
- Ⓕ TL 856 079
- Ⓖ TL 850 073

A combination of busy quaysides and boatyards, marinas and quiet river and canalside meadows, plus extensive views across the Blackwater Estuary, makes for an exceptionally enjoyable and varied walk. The route also passes through the centre of Maldon, a delightful old town well worth exploring. Much of the walk is beside water: either the Blackwater Estuary, River Chelmer or the Chelmer and Blackwater Navigation.

Begin by facing the estuary and heading across to the far right corner of the car park. Turn right along a tarmac track, turn left to the riverside promenade and turn left along it. Ahead is a superb view of Hythe Quay and St Mary's Church.

The quay was at its height in the 17th and 18th centuries when Maldon was a major port and it is still used today by some of the Thames sailing barges. St Mary's Church dates from the late 12th century but the original tower fell down in 1596 and was rebuilt in brick in 1636. The distinctive octagonal spire, added in 1740, was a valuable landmark for sailors navigating the Blackwater Estuary.

The promenade curves right between the river and a pool and emerges on to a road. Turn left Ⓐ beside the **Jolly Sailor Inn**, passing to the right of St Mary's Church, turn right at a T-junction into Maldon town centre and walk up High Street. Most of the town's main historic buildings are in High Street, and you pass – in order – the early 18th-century Plume Library, built on the site of the medieval St Peter's Church, the 15th-century Moot Hall, and the 13th-century All Saints' Church.

At All Saints' Church, turn right Ⓑ along Silver Street, which curves left and continues as Beeleigh Road. Where the road ends, keep ahead along a track but almost immediately bear slightly left to continue along a parallel, enclosed path, which later heads gently downhill under a green canopy to a stile. In order to avoid crossing the busy A414, turn right just before the stile onto a tarmac path which descends towards the River Chelmer and curves left to pass under a road bridge beside the river. The path then curves left again and heads up through trees to a T-junction. Turn right along an enclosed path, climb a stile and keep ahead across an enclosed grassy area to climb another stile in the left-hand corner. Continue along an enclosed path, passing to the left of Beeleigh Abbey, a private house built on the site of a 12th-century Premonstratensian monastery.

Continue along a tree-lined tarmac drive to a narrow lane **C**, turn right and, where the lane ends, keep ahead along a hedge- and tree-lined track. After this track bends right, keep ahead through a metal kissing-gate and along a wooded path to cross a footbridge over the River Chelmer by a weir. Turn right beside the river, past a redundant kissing-gate to reach the Chelmer and Blackwater Navigation by a lock, turn right on to a tarmac path and cross a bridge by another weir. The complex of waterways around here is known as the Beeleigh Falls.

Passing to the right of a brick bridge, continue along a tarmac track beside the Chelmer and Blackwater Navigation, opened in 1797 to provide a direct link between Chelmsford and the sea. To the right is Maldon golf course and, where the track bears right to the club house, keep ahead along a path beside the canal and turn left over the next bridge **D**. Turn right along the other bank and go under the bypass.

You now keep beside the canal to where it empties into the Blackwater Estuary at Heybridge Basin, a distance of about 2 miles (3.2km). At first the route is through the outskirts of the town, passing by industrial estates, but later the surroundings become more rural. At Heybridge Basin, turn right **E** to cross the lock gates and walk along an embankment by the estuary. Follow the river around a right-hand bend and continue along the embank-

ment, between the estuary on the left and a lake formed from a flooded gravel pit on the right. There are fine views across the water to Maldon. Beyond the lake, the path continues past a housing development, eventually turning out onto a road. Follow it left to a main road **F** and keep ahead to a mini-roundabout. Turn left back into Maldon – keeping ahead all the time and following signs to Town Centre, and after crossing the bridge over the River Chelmer, turn left **G** along Fullbridge Quay, passing boats and cranes.

Keep left along Chandlers Quay and, where the road ends, keep ahead – first along an enclosed path and later a tarmac drive – to emerge into Downs Road. Keep ahead to a crossroads and continue along The Hythe. At the Jolly Sailor Inn **A** you pick up the outward route and retrace your steps back to the starting point at Promenade Park. ●

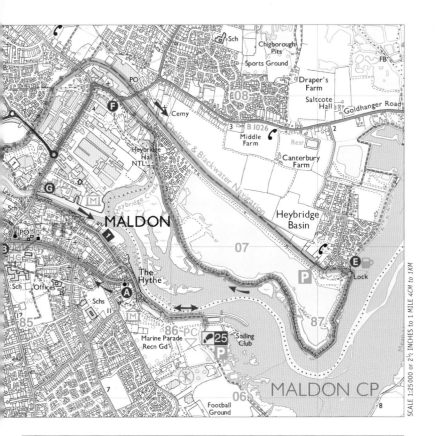

Maldon

White Notley and Cressing

White Notley and Cressing

		GPS waypoints	
Start	Cressing station, off Burford Mill Lane signposted from B1018 south of Braintree	🥾	TL 776 202
		A	TL 781 201
Distance	9½ miles (15km)	**B**	TL 772 195
Height gain	530 feet (160m)	**C**	TL 783 185
Approximate time	4½ hours	**D**	TL 787 184
		E	TL 799 185
Parking	Parking area by Cressing station, on west side of level crossing	**F**	TL 788 201
		G	TL 792 209
Ordnance Survey maps	Landranger 167 (Chelmsford), Explorers 195 (Braintree & Saffron Walden) and 183 (Chelmsford & The Rodings)	**H**	TL 778 211

This is a lengthy but relatively undemanding walk, mainly along well-signed tracks, field paths and quiet lanes, in the pleasant countryside of the Brain Valley to the south of Braintree. It passes through two attractive villages, both with traditional Essex churches, and includes a detour to the interesting Cressing Temple.

🥾 Turn right out of the parking area to go over the level crossing and walk along the lane to a T-junction. Turn right, in the Witham direction, and at a public footpath sign just before a farm **A**, turn sharp right over a stile and walk along the right-hand edge of a field. Go through a hedge gap, cross a track, go over a stile and head across a field to go through a kissing-gate in the middle bearing right before the field corner to a stile.

Climb the stile, cross a railway line, climb the stile opposite and continue gently downhill across a golf course. Cross a ditch, turn right, then turn left at a waymarked fingerpost to cross the second footbridge over the little River Brain and keep ahead to pick up a grassy path which continues gently uphill across the golf course to a stile by another fingerpost. After climbing it,

keep ahead across a field and climb another stile on to a road at The Green **B**. Turn right but, almost immediately, leave left along a track beside a house. Continue across the field behind, joining a ditch on the right.

The way zigzags towards the buildings of Webb's Farm, seen ahead, finally swinging left to come out on to Pole Lane. Turn right and take the first track on the left. The track winds between fields and, about 50 yards after passing a barn on the right, turn left at a waymarked post on to a concrete track, which later continues as a pleasant grassy track along the left-hand edge of fields. The track eventually becomes tree-lined and bends left to a fork. Take the right-hand track to emerge on to a road and turn right **C** into White Notley, an attractive village with a fine medieval church. At a

T-junction, turn left along a lane, in the Silver End and Cressing direction, and cross a bridge over the River Brain .

At this point, those wishing to cut short the walk should keep ahead along the lane; and follow the route description from the next time  *is shown in the text.*

For the full walk, immediately turn right – here joining the Essex Way – head across grass and continue along a track to a metal kissing-gate. Go through, walk along a straight, hedge-lined tarmac track, climb a stile and continue along the left-hand edge of a field. Climb another stile, walk along the left-hand edge of the next field and keep ahead, passing a footbridge over the River Brain, to a waymarked post. Turn left here and head gently uphill along the right-hand edge of a field, climb a stile and recross the railway line. Climb the stile opposite, keep ahead to go through a kissing-gate and walk across the next field and through another kissing-gate to emerge on to a road opposite Cressing Temple. Climb the stile opposite, turn right along a fence-lined path and turn left to the entrance .

Cressing Temple originally belonged to the Knights Templars but after the

On the banks of the little River Brain near Cressing Temple

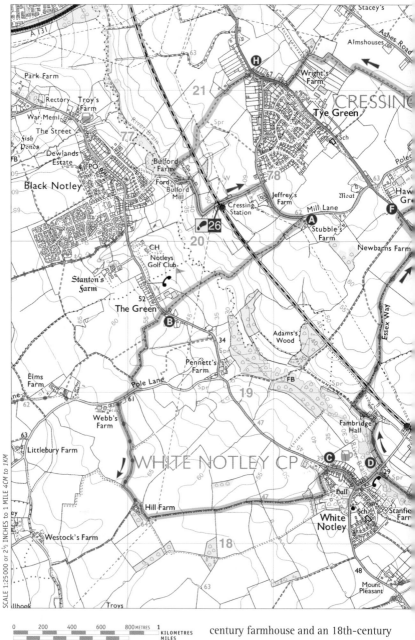

order was suppressed by the Pope in 1308, it passed to the Knights Hospitallers. The present complex of buildings includes two of the finest medieval timbered barns in Europe, plus an Elizabethan Court Hall, early 17th-century farmhouse and an 18th-century Waggon Lodge. There is also a walled garden and moats. Since 1987 it has been owned by Essex County Council.

Retrace your steps to the lane by the bridge over the river **D** and turn right. At a public footpath sign, turn left along the enclosed, tarmac track to Fambridge Hall and turn left at a

on in a straight line to emerge on to a lane in front of Cressing's medieval church. The church has a Norman nave and 13th-century chancel.

Turn left into Cressing, keep ahead past the village green along The Street and, at a public footpath sign where the road forks **G**, turn left along an enclosed path beside a field. Keep ahead into the next field but immediately turn right over a plank footbridge and continue along the right-hand field edge. In the corner, turn right through a kissing-gate and turn left, continuing initially by the left-hand field edge but bearing right away from it to go through another kissing-gate. Keep along the left-hand edge of the next two fields, by a ditch on the left. Follow the ditch around a left-hand bend and cross a footbridge over it. Turn right, continuing between a fence on the left and the ditch on the right, and the path turns first left and then right. After crossing a footbridge into trees, turn left along an enclosed path and bear left to join a track. Keep ahead over a crossing farm track to come out on to a road on the edge of Tye Green.

Turn right, continuing past Mill Lane but then, at a public footpath sign, turn left **H** along an enclosed, tarmac track. Pass beside a vehicle scrapyard, keep ahead to climb a stile and continue across a field, making for a pylon where there is a waymarked post. Bear left to head across to the field corner, climb a stile, cross the railway line for the last time, climb another stile and head downhill along the left-hand field edge.

At the bottom, turn left along an enclosed path, passing to the left of Bulford Mill, climb a stile and keep ahead to a lane. Turn left uphill and follow the lane around right- and left-hand bends to return to the starting point at Cressing Station.

T-junction by the hall to continue along a gently descending track. Turn right along a track at an Essex Way post, pass under a railway bridge and the track winds across fields to a farm. Turn left here through a hedge gap, and go right, out to a road. Cross the road and walk left for 200 yards to find a path leaving on the right **F**. Entering a field, carry

Epping Forest and Upshire

		GPS waypoints
Start	High Beach, Epping Forest Centre, signposted from A121	🥾 TQ 412 981
Distance	8¾ miles (14km)	Ⓐ TQ 420 977
Height gain	610 feet (185m)	Ⓑ TL 450 010
Approximate time	4½ hours	Ⓒ TL 446 010
Parking	Epping Forest Centre	Ⓓ TL 422 014
Ordnance Survey maps	Landranger 167 (Chelmsford), Explorer 174 (Epping Forest & Lee Valley)	Ⓔ TL 417 010
		Ⓕ TQ 420 994
		Ⓖ TQ 414 988

Approximately three quarters of this walk is through the splendid woodlands at the northern end of Epping Forest, once part of the vast royal hunting grounds of the Forest of Essex. At about the halfway point at Bell Common, you emerge from the forest and continue across more open country, enjoying extensive views, to the village of Upshire. You then plunge back into woodland for the final stretch. Route finding is generally easy except perhaps at the start, where you need to follow the directions carefully in order to reach the Green Ride, a clearly defined track through the forest.

During the Middle Ages, the Forest of Essex, subsequently known as Waltham Forest, covered much of the county, and its proximity to the capital made it one of the most popular of royal hunting grounds. From the 17th century onwards, fellings and enclosures caused it to shrink rapidly and it became fragmented. The present Epping Forest is the largest of the remaining fragments, covering nearly 6,000 acres (2,430 hectares) and comprising mainly hornbeam, oak, beech and birch. It was fortunately saved from further destruction by the Corporation of the City of London. By an Act of Parliament in 1878, the Corporation became the Conservators of Epping Forest in order to preserve it 'as an open space for the recreation and enjoyment of the public'.

In the 18th century, Epping Forest was a favourite haunt of the notorious highwayman Dick Turpin.

🥾 Begin by taking the path between the Visitor Centre on the right and the Field Studies Centre on the left and continue along a path that curves right by a small pool on the right and then descend steps to go through a gate. Turn left alongside the boundary fence of the Epping Forest Centre and, at the fence corner, keep ahead to a T-junction. Turn left along a track and, just before it bears slightly left, turn right on to a path that descends to a road.

Cross over, keep ahead to a three-way junction and take the left-hand path, heading slightly uphill and then curving right to continue through the trees, keeping more or less in a straight

Epping Forest

line, to reach a sandy track in a clearing. Turn left along the track **A** – this is the Green Ride – and, ignoring all side turns, follow it through the superb woodlands of Great Monk Wood to reach a road. Cross it and, passing to the right of a small car park, continue along the track opposite, descending and then rising to reach a T-junction. Turn left along a track to go through a car park on to a road.

Cross over, go through another car park, pass beside a barrier and take the broad track ahead. Keep on the main track all the time to pass to the right of the tree-covered earthworks of Ambresbury Banks, an Iron Age defence. Continue along an undulating track, which eventually passes beside a

barrier to emerge from the forest and keeps ahead to a road **B**. Turn left, and the road curves left to a T-junction at Bell Common. Turn left, in the Woodford direction. After ¼ mile (400m), at a public footpath sign, bear right on to an enclosed path **C**.

The path bears right to a ladder-stile beside the M25. After climbing it, the right-of-way continues over the stile immediately in front and across a field, turning left down to the field edge and turning right along it. Bear left to go through a squeezer stile in the field corner and turn right along the right-hand edge of the next field, beside Griffin's Wood. At the corner of the wood, bear left at a waymarked fingerpost by a gate, to continue along

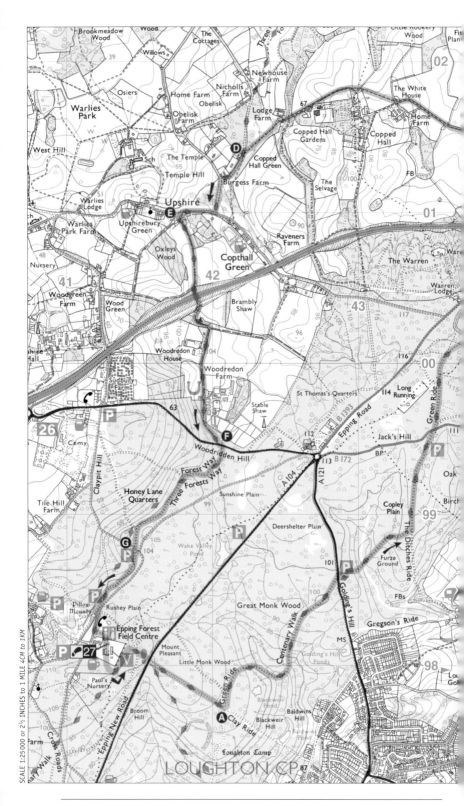

SCALE 1:25000 or 2½ INCHES to 1 MILE 4CM to 1KM

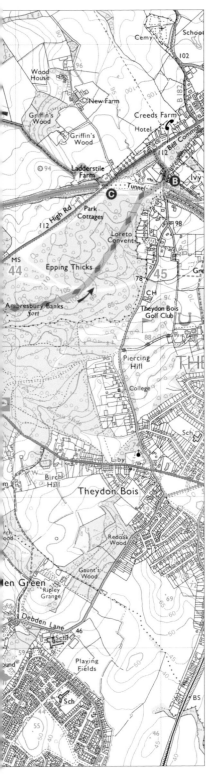

the right-hand edge of the next two fields. At the second field corner go through a squeezer stile onto a tarmac drive and turn left. The drive heads gently uphill and curves left at the top to reach a crossroads.

Turn right, almost immediately turn left over a stile, at a public footpath sign, and walk diagonally across a field. On the far side, pass through a hedge gap and cross a plank footbridge. Bear left to head across the corner of the next field to join a tarmac track at a bend and keep along the track to a T-junction just beyond a gate. Turn left to a lane **D**. Go left along the lane to a T-junction and turn left again at the end (Long Street) to another T-junction.

Turn right into Upshire keeping ahead past a triangular green **E** to visit the church and **The Horseshoes** pub. Although the church looks traditional, with the usual Essex timber bell turret, it was only built in 1902.

Return to the green **E** and now bear right, passing through a gate to follow a track onto the Woodredon and Warlies Park Estate, shortly crossing the M25. Keep ahead uphill, follow the track around a left-hand bend and, at a fork, take the right-hand track, signposted Forest Way. After passing the imposing Woodredon House on the right, the track becomes a tarmac one and you continue along it, passing beside a gate and on through trees to a road **F**.

Turn left and almost immediately turn right along a winding track towards Loughton. Cross over the next road **G**, pass beside a barrier and continue along a track to emerge on to another road at a junction. Take the road ahead, which leads back to the **King's Oak** pub and the entrance to the Epping Forest Centre. ⬤

St Peter's Chapel, Bradwell Marshes and Tillingham

St Peter's Chapel, Bradwell Marshes and Tillingham

		GPS waypoints
Start	St Nicholas Church, Tillingham	🖋 TL 992 038
Distance	9¾ miles (15.6km)	**Ⓐ** TL 998 048
Height gain	155 feet (45m)	**Ⓑ** TL 997 062
Approximate time	4½ hours	**Ⓒ** TM 004 068
Parking	Village car park opposite St Nicholas Church, Tillingham	**Ⓓ** TM 030 081
		Ⓔ TM 029 051
Ordnance Survey maps	Landranger 168 (Colchester), Explorer 176 (Blackwater Estuary)	**Ⓕ** TM 014 052

Nowhere else in Essex do you experience the sense of remoteness and isolation as on this lengthy walk, much of which is across the lonely and desolate marshland of the Dengie Peninsula, which lies between the Blackwater and Crouch estuaries. Even the nuclear power station at Bradwell hardly intrudes on this otherwise unspoilt scene. The highlight of the walk is the isolated and tiny Saxon chapel of St Peter-on-the-Wall but the route also passes through two villages, both of which have medieval churches and possess at least one pub. Tillingham, where the walk begins, is a most appealing village, with weather-boarded cottages around a green presided over by the fine 12th- to 14th-century church.

🖋 Out of the car park, cross the road and enter the churchyard. Walk around the church past its south front and turn left on a path past the east end to a kissing-gate at the far side of the grave yard. Through that, turn right past the graveyard into the corner of a field. Keep ahead beside the boundary on a field path, putting the hedge on your left. After a good ¼ mile (400m), reaching a crossing track, go left through a belt of trees and continue between open fields to Mark Farm. Approaching the outbuildings, bear right into the yard. Cross and follow a track away to the left, which leads out to a narrow lane **Ⓐ**.

Go right shortly reaching a farm, Packards. Turn left to continue along a track. Bear left through a spinney, cross a footbridge by a waymarked post and keep ahead along a narrow path through trees and bushes to emerge into a field. The way now is straight ahead across the field to a stile.

Climb the stile, keep ahead through trees, climb another stile on the far side and continue across a field. After going through a hedge gap to the right of a row of telegraph poles, walk along the right-hand edge of the next field to a lane **Ⓑ**. Turn right and keep with the main lane winding into Bradwell-on-Sea, some ¾ mile (1.2km) away. As its name indicates, the village was once on the coast but the sea has receded, leaving it nearly 2 miles inland (3.2km). The 14th-century church has a west tower built of brick in 1706.

Just before reaching the **Kings Head** and the church, turn off right into East End Road **G**. Keep ahead along this quiet residential road and soon Bradwell Power Station comes into view to the left. Continue along the lane for about 1½ miles (2.4km), passing **St Cedds Café** and the entrance to a caravan site, to its end by Eastlands Farm. Keep ahead along a track, go through a kissing-gate and continue to the Saxon chapel of St Peter-on-the-Wall **D**.

This tiny and highly atmospheric church, situated amid lonely marshes and overlooking the North Sea, was founded by St Cedd in the 7th century. St Cedd was a priest at Lindisfarne, or Holy Island, on the Northumberland coast who came to St Peters-on-the-Wall to preach Christianity. The church stands on the site of the 3rd-century Roman fort of Othona, and stones from the fort were used in its construction. In the later Middle Ages the population moved away to the village of Bradwell-on-Sea and the chapel became abandoned and redundant. For several centuries it was used as a barn but in 1920 it was restored and rededicated.

The track swings right in front of the chapel and, on reaching an embankment, head up on to it and turn right. You now continue along the top of this embankment above the wide and desolate Bradwell Marshes for the next 2 miles (3.2km), following it around a bulge – turning first left, then right (now closer to the sea), right again and left again. Where the embankment next turns left, bear right at a waymarked post to descend from it and continue

The isolated and tiny Saxon chapel of St Peter-on-the-Wall

along a concrete track. At the next waymarked post, turn right **E** along a track and, where it turns right to a farm, keep ahead to climb two stiles. After climbing the second stile, walk across a field, keeping parallel to its right-hand edge, and make for a stile in the right-hand corner. Climb it, keep along the left-hand edge of the next field – above a ditch – this area may be overgrown so follow the ditch first to the left and then to the right and continue across fields, bearing left to a waymarked post 50 yards to the right of an old farm building **F**. Cross a causeway between channels, keep to the right of the old farm building and then bear left around it. Where the wall ends turn right and head straight across the field crossing a ditch at a waymarked post. Keep ahead across the next field, on the far side of which go through a hedge gap to join a track.

Follow the track right around a left-hand bend but almost immediately turn right to cross a footbridge. Head diagonally across a field, go through a hedge gap by a waymarked post to rejoin the previous track and continue along it towards a farm. After passing through the farm, keep ahead along a lane and, where it turns left, continue along the right-hand edge of a field.

After going over a crossing track, Tillingham church comes into view. Retrace your outward route along the field edge and through the churchyard back to the start. ●

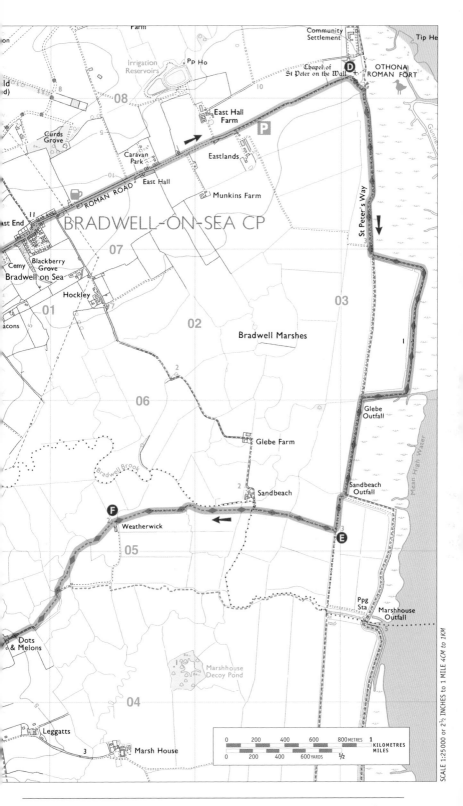

SCALE 1:25000 or 2½ INCHES to 1 MILE 4CM to 1KM

| 0 | 200 | 400 | 600 | 800 METRES | 1 |
| 0 | 200 | 400 | 600 YARDS | ½ | KILOMETRES MILES |

Further Information

 ### The National Trust

Anyone who likes visiting places of natural beauty and/or historic interest has cause to be grateful to the National Trust. Without it, many such places would probably have vanished by now.

It was in response to the pressures on the countryside posed by the relentless march of Victorian industrialisation that the trust was set up in 1895. Its founders, inspired by the common goals of protecting and conserving Britain's national heritage and widening public access to it, were Sir Robert Hunter, Octavia Hill and Canon Rawnsley: respectively a solicitor, a social reformer and a clergyman. The latter was particularly influential. As a canon of Carlisle Cathedral and vicar of Crosthwaite (near Keswick), he was concerned about threats to the Lake District and had already been active in protecting footpaths and promoting public access to open countryside. After the flooding of Thirlmere in 1879 to create a large reservoir, he became increasingly convinced that the only effective way to guarantee protection was outright ownership of land.

The purpose of the National Trust is to preserve areas of natural beauty and sites of historic interest by acquisition, holding them in trust for the nation and making them available for public access and enjoyment. Some of its properties have been acquired through purchase, but many of the Trust's properties have been donated. Nowadays it is not only one of the biggest landowners in the country, but also one of the most active conservation charities, protecting 618,000 acres (just over 250,000ha) of land, including 775 miles (1,240km) of coastline, and over 300 historic properties in England, Wales and Northern Ireland. (There is a separate National Trust for Scotland, founded in 1931.)

Furthermore, once a piece of land has come under National Trust ownership, it is difficult for its status to be altered. As a result of parliamentary legislation in 1907, the Trust was given the right to declare its property inalienable, so ensuring that in any subsequent dispute it can appeal directly to parliament.

As it works towards its dual aims of conserving areas of attractive countryside and encouraging greater public access (not easy to reconcile in this age of mass tourism), the Trust provides an excellent service for walkers by creating new concessionary paths and waymarked trails, maintaining stiles and foot bridges and combating the ever-increasing problem of footpath erosion.

For details of membership, contact the National Trust at the address on page 95.

 ### The Ramblers

No organisation works more actively to protect and extend the rights and interests of walkers in the countryside than the Ramblers. Its aims are clear: to foster a greater knowledge, love and care of the countryside; to assist in the protection and enhancement of public rights of way and areas of natural beauty; to work for greater public access to the countryside; and to encourage more people to take up rambling as a healthy, recreational leisure activity.

It was founded in 1935 when, following the setting up of a National Council of Ramblers' Federations in 1931, a number of federations earlier formed in London, Manchester, the Midlands and elsewhere came together to create a more effective pressure group, to deal with such problems as the disappearance and obstruction of footpaths, the prevention of access to open mountain and moorland and increasing hostility from landowners. This was the era of the mass trespasses, when there were sometimes violent

On the cliffs at The Naze

confrontations between ramblers and gamekeepers, especially on the moorlands of the Peak District.

Since then the Ramblers has played an influential role in preserving and developing the national footpath network, supporting the creation of national parks and encouraging the designation and waymarking of long-distance routes.

Our freedom to walk in the countryside is precarious and requires constant vigilance. As well as the perennial problems of footpaths being illegally obstructed, disappearing through lack of use or extinguished by housing or road construction, new dangers can spring up at any time.

It is to meet such problems and dangers that the Ramblers exists and represents the interests of all walkers. The address to write to for information on the Ramblers and how to become a member is given on page 95.

 Walkers and the Law

The *Countryside and Rights of Way Act 2000 (CRoW)* gives a public right of access in England and Wales to land mapped as open country (mountain, moor, heath and down) or registered common land. These areas are known as *open access land*, and include land around the coastline, known as *coastal margin*.

Where You Can Go
Rights of Way
Prior to the introduction of *CRoW* walkers could only legally access the countryside along public rights of way. These are either 'footpaths' (for walkers only) or 'bridleways' (for walkers, riders on horseback and pedal cyclists). A third category called 'Byways open to all traffic' (BOATs), is used by motorised vehicles as well as those using non-mechanised transport. Mainly they are green lanes, farm and estate roads, although occasionally they will be found crossing mountainous area.

Rights of way are marked on Ordnance Survey maps. Look for the green broken lines on the Explorer maps, or the red dashed lines on Landranger maps.

The term 'right of way' means exactly what it says. It gives a right of passage over what, for the most part, is private land. Under pre-CRoW legislation walkers were required to keep to the line of the right of way and not stray onto land on either side. If you did inadvertently wander off the right of way, either because of faulty map reading or because the route was not clearly indicated on the ground,

Countryside Access Charter

Your rights of way are:

- public footpaths – on foot only. Sometimes waymarked in yellow
- bridleways – on foot, horseback and pedal cycle. Sometimes waymarked in blue
- byways (usually old roads), most 'roads used as public paths' and, of course, public roads – all traffic has the right of way

Use maps, signs and waymarks to check rights of way. Ordnance Survey Explorer and Landranger maps show most public rights of way

On rights of way you can:

- take a pram, pushchair or wheelchair if practicable
- take a dog (on a lead or under close control)
- take a short route round an illegal obstruction or remove it sufficiently to get past

You have a right to go for recreation to:

- public parks and open spaces – on foot
- most commons near older towns and cities – on foot and sometimes on horseback
- private land where the owner has a formal agreement with the local authority

In addition you can use the following by local or established custom or consent, but ask for advice if you are unsure:

- many areas of open country, such as moorland, fell and coastal areas, especially those in the care of the National Trust, and some commons
- some woods and forests, especially those owned by the Forestry Commission
- country parks and picnic sites
- most beaches
- canal towpaths
- some private paths and tracks Consent sometimes extends to horse-riding and cycling

For your information:

- county councils and London boroughs maintain and record rights of way, and register commons
- obstructions, dangerous animals, harassment and misleading signs on rights of way are illegal and you should report them to the county council
- paths across fields can be ploughed, but must normally be reinstated within two weeks
- landowners can require you to leave land to which you have no right of access
- motor vehicles are normally permitted only on roads, byways and some 'roads used as public paths'

you were technically trespassing.

Local authorities have a legal obligation to ensure that rights of way are kept clear and free of obstruction, and are signposted where they leave metalled roads. The duty of local authorities to install signposts extends to the placing of signs along a path or way, but only where the authority considers it necessary to have a signpost or waymark to assist persons unfamiliar with the locality.

CRoW Access Rights
Access Land

As well as being able to walk on existing rights of way, under CRoW legislation you have access to large areas of open land and, under further legislation, a right of

coastal access, which is being implemented by Natural England, giving for the first time the right of access around all England's open coast. This includes plans for an England Coast Path (ECP) which will run for 2,795 miles (4,500 kilometres). A corresponding Wales Coast Path has been open since 2012.

Coastal access rights apply within the coastal margin (including along the ECP) unless the land falls into a category of excepted land or is subject to local restrictions, exclusions or diversions.

You can of course continue to use rights of way to cross access land, but you can lawfully leave the path and wander at will in these designated areas.

Where to Walk

Access Land is shown on Ordnance Survey Explorer maps by a light yellow tint surrounded by a pale orange border. New orange coloured 'i' symbols on the maps will show the location of permanent access information boards installed by the access authorities. Coastal Margin is shown on Ordnance Survey Explorer maps by a pink tint.

Restrictions

The right to walk on access land may lawfully be restricted by landowners. Landowners can, for any reason, restrict access for up to 28 days in any year. They cannot however close the land:

- on bank holidays;
- for more than four Saturdays and Sundays in a year;
- on any Saturday from 1 June to 11 August; or
- on any Sunday from 1 June to the end of September.

They have to provide local authorities with five working days' notice before the date of closure unless the land involved is an area of less than five hectares or the closure is for less than four hours. In these cases landowners only need to provide two hours' notice.

Whatever restrictions are put into place on access land they have no effect on existing rights of way, and you can continue to walk on them.

Dogs

Dogs can be taken on access land, but must be kept on leads of two metres or less between 1 March and 31 July, and at all times where they are near livestock. In addition landowners may impose a ban on all dogs from fields where lambing takes place for up to six weeks in any year. Dogs may be banned from moorland used for grouse shooting and breeding for up to five years.

In the main, walkers following the routes in this book will continue to follow existing rights of way, but a knowledge and understanding of the law as it affects walkers, plus the ability to distinguish

access land marked on the maps, will enable anyone who wishes to depart from paths that cross access land either to take a shortcut, to enjoy a view or to explore.

General Obstructions

Obstructions can sometimes cause a problem on a walk and the most common of these is where the path across a field has been ploughed over. It is legal for a farmer to plough up a path provided that it is restored within two weeks. This does not always happen and you are faced with the dilemma of following the line of the path, even if this means treading on crops, or walking round the edge of the field. Although the later course of action seems the most sensible, it does mean that you would be trespassing.

Other obstructions can vary from overhanging vegetation to wire fences across the path, locked gates or even a cattle feeder on the path.

Use common sense. If you can get round the obstruction without causing damage, do so. Otherwise only remove as much of the obstruction as is necessary to secure passage.

If the right of way is blocked and cannot be followed, there is a long-standing view that in such circumstances there is a right to deviate, but this cannot wholly be relied on. Although it is accepted in law that highways (and that includes rights of way) are for the public service, and if the usual track is impassable, it is for the general good that people should be entitled to pass into another line. However, this should not be taken as indicating a right to deviate whenever a way becomes impassable. If in doubt, retreat.

Report obstructions to the local authority and/or the Ramblers.

 Global Positioning System (GPS)

What is GPS?

GPS is a worldwide radio navigation system that uses a network of at least 24 satellites and receivers, usually hand-held, to calculate positions. By measuring the time it takes a signal to reach the receiver, the distance from the satellite can be estimated. Repeat this with several satellites and the receiver can then use triangulation to establish the position of the receiver.

How to use GPS with Ordnance Survey mapping

Each of the walks in this book includes GPS co-ordinate data that reflects the walk position points on Ordnance Survey maps.

GPS and OS maps use different models for the earth and co-ordinate systems, so when you are trying to relate your GPS position to features on the map the two will differ slightly. This is especially the case with height, as the model that relates the GPS global co-ordinate system to height above sea level is very poor.

When using GPS with OS mapping, some distortion – up to 16ft (5m) – will always be present. Moreover, individual features on maps may have been surveyed only to an accuracy of 23ft (7m) (for 1:25000 scale maps), while other features, e.g. boulders, are usually only shown schematically.

In practice, this should not cause undue difficulty, as you will be near enough to your objective to be able to spot it.

How to use the GPS data in this book

There are various ways you can use the GPS data in this book.

1. Follow the route description while checking your position on your receiver when you are approaching a position point.

2. You can also use the positioning information on your receiver to verify where you are on the map.

3. Alternatively, you can use some of the proprietary software that is available. At the simple end there is inexpensive software, which lets you input the walk positions (waypoints), download them to the gps unit and then use them to assist your navigation on the walks.

At the upper end of the market Ordnance Survey maps are available in electronic form. Most come with software

that enables you to enter your walking route onto the map, download it to your gps unit and use it, alongside the route description, to follow the route.

Walking Safety

Although the reasonably gentle country-side that is the subject of this book offers no real dangers to walkers at any time of the year, it is still advisable to take sensible precautions and follow certain well-tried guidelines.

Always take with you both warm and waterproof clothing and sufficient food and drink. Wear suitable footwear, such as strong walking boots or shoes that give a good grip over stony ground, on slippery slopes and in muddy conditions. Try to obtain a local weather forecast and bear it in mind before you start. Do not be afraid to abandon your proposed route and return to your starting point in the event of a sudden and unexpected deterioration in the weather.

All the walks described in this book will be safe to do, given due care and respect, even during the winter. Indeed, a crisp, fine winter day often provides perfect walking conditions, with firm ground underfoot and a clarity unique to this time of the year.

The most difficult hazard likely to be encountered is mud, especially when walking along woodland and field paths, farm tracks and bridleways – the latter in particular can often get churned up by cyclists and horses. In summer, an additional difficulty may be narrow and overgrown paths, particularly along the edges of cultivated fields. Neither should constitute a major problem provided that the appropriate footwear is worn.

Useful Organisations

Campaign to Protect Rural England
5-11 Lavington Street,
London SE1 0NZ

Tel. 0207 981 2800
www.cpre.org.uk

Essex County Council
County Hall, Market Road,
Chelmsford, Essex CM1 1QH.
Tel. 0345 743 0430
www.essex.gov.uk

Essex Wildlife Trust
Abbotts Hall Farm,
Gt Wigborough, Colchester,
Essex CO5 7RZ.
Tel. 01621 862960
www.essexwt.org.uk

Forestry Commission East Anglia
Santon Downham, Brandon,
Suffolk IP27 0TJ.
Tel. 0300 067 4574
www.forestry.gov.uk

Long Distance Walkers' Association
www.ldwa.org.uk

National Trust
Membership and general enquiries:
Tel. 0344 800 1895
www.nationaltrust.org.uk
East of England
Westley Bottom, Bury St Edmunds,
Suffolk IP33 3WD.
Tel. 01284 747 500

Natural England
Tel. 0300 060 3900
www.gov.uk/government/organisations/n
atural-england

Ordnance Survey
Tel. 03456 05 05 05 (Lo-call)
www.ordnancesurvey.co.uk

Ramblers
2nd Floor, Camelford House,
87–90 Albert Embankment,
London SE1 7TW.
Tel. 020 7339 8500
www.ramblers.org.uk

East of England Tourism
www.visiteastofengland.com

Local tourist information offices:
Braintree: 01376 550066
Brentwood: 01277 200300
Clacton: 01255 686633
Colchester: 01206 282920
Maldon: 01621 856503
Saffron Walden: 01799 524022
Southend-on-Sea: 01702 618747
Waltham Abbey: 01992 660336
Witham: 01376 502674

Youth Hostels Association
Trevelyan House, Dimple Road,
Matlock, Derbyshire
DE4 3YH.
Tel. 01629 592700
www.yha.org.uk

 Ordnance Survey
Maps of Essex

The area of Essex is covered by Ordnance
Survey 1:50 000 (1¼ inches to 1 mile or
2cm to 1km) scale Landranger map sheets
154, 155, 166, 167, 168, 169, 177, 178.
These all-purpose maps are packed with
information to help you explore the area.
Viewpoints, picnic sites, places of interest
and caravan and camping sites are shown,
as well as public rights of way information
such as footpaths and bridleways.

To examine the Essex area in more detail,
and especially if you are planning walks,
Ordnance Survey Explorer maps at
1:25 000 (2½ inches to 1 mile or 4cm to
1km) scale are ideal. Maps covering this
area are:

174 Epping Forest & Lee Valley
175 Southend–on–Sea & Basildon
176 Blackwater Estuary
183 Chelmsford & The Rodings
184 Colchester
195 Braintree & Saffron Walden
196 Sudbury, Hadleigh & Dedham Vale

Ordnance Survey maps and guides are
available from most booksellers, stationers
and newsagents.

Ordnance Survey

Scotland
Pathfinder Walks
3 ISLE OF SKYE
4 CAIRNGORMS
7 FORT WILLIAM & GLEN COE
19 DUMFRIES & GALLOWAY
23 LOCH LOMOND, THE TROSSACHS, & STIRLING
27 PERTHSHIRE, ANGUS & FIFE
30 LOCH NESS & INVERNESS
31 OBAN, MULL & KINTYRE
46 ABERDEEN & ROYAL DEESIDE
47 EDINBURGH, PENTLANDS & LOTHIANS

North of England
Pathfinder Walks
15 YORKSHIRE DALES
22 MORE LAKE DISTRICT
28 NORTH YORK MOORS
35 NORTHUMBERLAND & SCOTTISH BORDERS
39 DURHAM, NORTH PENNINES & TYNE AND WEAR
42 CHESHIRE
49 VALE OF YORK & YORKSHIRE WOLDS
53 LANCASHIRE
60 LAKE DISTRICT
63 PEAK DISTRICT
64 SOUTH PENNINES
71 THE HIGH FELLS OF LAKELAND
73 MORE PEAK DISTRICT
Short Walks
1 YORKSHIRE DALES
2 PEAK DISTRICT
3 LAKE DISTRICT
13 NORTH YORK MOORS

Wales
Pathfinder Walks
10 SNOWDONIA
18 BRECON BEACONS
32 NORTH WALES & SNOWDONIA
34 PEMBROKESHIRE & CARMARTHENSHIRE
41 MID WALES
55 GOWER, SWANSEA & CARDIFF
Short Walks
14 SNOWDONIA
31 BRECON BEACONS

Heart of England
Pathfinder Walks
6 COTSWOLDS
14 SHROPSHIRE & STAFFORDSHIRE
20 SHERWOOD FOREST & THE EAST MIDLANDS
29 WYE VALLEY & FOREST OF DEAN
74 THE MALVERNS TO WARWICKSHIRE

Short Walks
4 COTSWOLDS
32 HEREFORDSHIRE & THE WYE VALLEY

East of England
Pathfinder Walks
44 ESSEX
45 NORFOLK
48 SUFFOLK
50 LINCOLNSHIRE & THE WOLDS
51 CAMBRIDGESHIRE & THE FENS
Short Walks
33 NORFOLK INTO SUFFOLK

South West of England
Pathfinder Walks
1 SOUTH DEVON & DARTMOOR
5 CORNWALL
9 EXMOOR & THE QUANTOCKS
11 DORSET & THE JURASSIC COAST
21 SOMERSET, THE MENDIPS & WILTSHIRE
26 DARTMOOR
68 NORTH & MID DEVON
69 SOUTH WEST ENGLAND'S COAST
Short Walks
8 DARTMOOR
9 CORNWALL
21 EXMOOR
29 SOUTH DEVON

South East of England
Pathfinder Walks
8 KENT
12 NEW FOREST, HAMPSHIRE & SOUTH DOWNS
25 THAMES VALLEY & CHILTERNS
54 HERTFORDSHIRE & BEDFORDSHIRE
65 SURREY
66 SOUTH DOWNS NATIONAL PARK & WEST SUSSEX
67 SOUTH DOWNS NATIONAL PARK & EAST SUSSEX
72 THE HOME COUNTIES FROM LONDON BY TRAIN
Short Walks
23 NEW FOREST NATIONAL PARK
27 ISLE OF WIGHT

Practical Guide
75 NAVIGATION SKILLS FOR WALKERS

City Walks
LONDON
OXFORD
EDINBURGH